A CRUISING GUIDE
—— TO THE ——
CARIBBEAN
From Antigua to Venezuela
MICHAEL W MARSHALL

ADLARD COLES NAUTICAL
London

For Julie and Sylvie
And all those I have sailed with

Published by Adlard Coles Nautical
An imprint of A & C Black (Publishers) Ltd
35 Bedford Row, London WC1R 4JH

Copyright © Michael W Marshall

First edition 1991

ISBN 0-7136-3452-9

A CIP catalogue record for this book is available from the British Library.

Typeset by Keepdate Ltd, Tyne & Wear
Printed and bound in Great Britain by Whitstable Litho, Whitstable

Acknowledgments
Special thanks are due to Mrs R Baker, Ms C Dubois, Ms J Hinves and Ms E Robson for their useful comments and help during the preparation of this book. Also Peter, my brother, who has crossed an ocean with me and shared my love of the sea since childhood.

CONTENTS

Preface

A Cruising Guide to the Caribbean provides all the information needed for those intending to charter a yacht in the Caribbean or those crossing the Atlantic to the islands for the first time. It describes all the important anchorages in the Caribbean island chain from Antigua in the north to Trinidad and Tobago. Also included are Barbados, as it is once again becoming an important first stop for west-bound, transatlantic yachts, and north east Venezuela where, in order to avoid the hurricane season, increasing numbers of yachts are spending the summer. There is no other English-language guide that, in one volume, covers such a large part of the Caribbean.

With charts and this guide the Caribbean islands and anchorages are ready to be explored. You will find them full of contrasts: quiet and crowded bays, flat and mountainous islands, sophisticated resorts and ramshackle towns, restaurants serving cordon bleu cooking and French champagne and shacks selling rotis and white lightning rum. But there is one constancy - the sea. Warm, clear, turquoise and blue, it washes the sun-bleached coral sand and is home to myriads of brightly coloured fish. The steady trade winds rustle the palm trees, cool the anchorages and drive sailing boats through sparkling seas.

When you first arrive from the crowded polluted anchorages of the Mediterranean or the dull uncertain weather of northern Europe, the Caribbean anchorages seem like Paradise - for most the feeling never leaves. But some, who have known the anchorages for years, resent the increasing numbers of charter boats, the crowded bays, the harpooned fish, the absent lobsters and conch, found now only in deep water, and of course the tourist developments. But if you sail out of season the anchorages are deserted, the developments are often well done and there are many uninhabited islands, or some islands where the steamer visits once or twice a week and where homes are still lit with paraffin lamps.

The fast, exhilarating sailing between the islands has to be experienced to be believed, and every island is criss-crossed with long lonely paths that suddenly give breathtaking views of the sea. In short come and join us - you will never regret it.

Key and List of Abbreviations

Chart Symbols	(ALL DEPTHS IN METRES)		Abbreviations
Safe anchorage	⚓		Flashing (Fl)
Conspic. palm trees	🌴		Group Flashing Three (3)
Green buoy		(G)	Occulting (Oc)
Red buoy		(R)	Fixed (F)
Yellow and Black IALA Buoy		(YB)	Metres (m)
Fixed light	✶		Miles (M)
Coral reef			Seconds (s)
Dangerous rocks	+		Depths in metres (5)
Mangrove trees			1000 Hertz (kHz)
Mountain peak	▲		

INTRODUCTION

Classical Caribbean anchorages

In this guide I have almost exclusively described 'classical' anchorages, many of which have been used by sailing craft from the Age of Discovery until the present day. Classical anchorages are often a convenient day's sail apart and they offer the best shelter from wind and sea. There are, of course, other less important anchorages in the region covered by this guide, but approaching them from the sea will always be more difficult and their shore-based facilities are usually non-existent. These minor anchorages are often worth exploring from the safe haven of a classical anchorage; some have been included.

A word of caution. *A Cruising Guide to the Caribbean* must, like all guides, be used in conjunction with large scale, good quality, up-to-date, official charts - especially important if you are visiting any island, anchorage (or marina) for the first time. While every effort has been made to produce an accurate, up-to-date guide neither the publishers nor the author are responsible for any errors or omissions in this guide. Also neither the publishers nor the author will accept any responsibility for any damage done to yourself, your boat, your crew or anyone or anything else. In other words, if you hit a rock using this guide it's your fault!

The dream and the reality

The Caribbean is a good place to buy a yacht. In the marinas, yacht clubs and chandleries there are many fine boats advertised for sale,

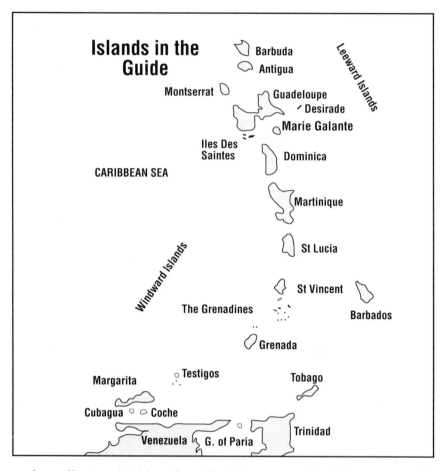

Islands in the Guide

Barbuda
Antigua
Leeward Islands
Montserrat
Guadeloupe
Desirade
Marie Galante
Iles Des Saintes
Dominica
CARIBBEAN SEA
Martinique
St Lucia
Windward Islands
St Vincent
The Grenadines
Barbados
Grenada
Margarita
Testigos
Tobago
Cubagua   Coche
Venezuela   G. of Paria
Trinidad

and usually at a third less than their European price. They come with Atlantic pilots, charts and self steering gears, but the skippers have all gone home - for them the reality did not match the dream. But the Caribbean is a yachting paradise. Warm, turquoise and emerald seas lap golden sanded bays and cruising yachts rest quietly at anchor under sun-drenched blue skies whilst, cooled by the trade winds, their crews idle away their days diving, swimming, windsurfing and toasting glorious sunsets with rum punches filled with crushed ice and exotic tropical fruits. So why does it all go wrong?

There is a French psychiatrist who lives aboard his yacht in a marina in Martinique. He makes a good living out of counselling couples who arrive at the marina after crossing the Atlantic. 'After one ocean crossing fifty per cent of the marriages end up in the divorce courts,' he says. 'Couples think that they just have to sell the house, walk on to their boat and sail away over the seas to Paradise. They have never tried living together in hot, damp, cramped conditions for weeks and months on end, with no release from each other's company.' He continues: 'Yachting magazines, yacht builders, the whole industry creates illusions about ocean sailing. The blue water dream sells yachts but it does not tell crews how to live on them. Ocean sailing can make a lot of people very scared and very unhappy.'

It is important to be scared - a skipper without fear is a bad skipper. For fear heightens awareness, speeds reflexes and helps decision making. But to be so scared that you shout at everyone and can never relax will ruin an ocean voyage. Often it is fear of fear that is the crippling emotion. It can bring about agonies of self doubt before the onset of a voyage or during a storm at sea, reducing physically strong people to a psychological state where they are unable to make good decisions or they lose the will to act. Can I cope with the responsibility? Will I be seasick? Will it be too rough for the boat? Will the engine start? Suppose the forestay parts or we lose a halyard; suppose there is fog; suppose we get lost; and so on.

Most accomplished sailors will have had practical experience of these worries so that their fear of fear will have been much reduced. These sailors make regular, safe, ocean passages and usually sail in simply-rigged, strongly built cruising yachts of around 12 m long with the minimum of electronic gear. They also have a strong determination to keep on sailing despite adverse changes in the weather. While most probably feel flutters of anxiety when they first set out from the shore, once they are away from the sight of land, and providing the weather is fine, anxiety subsides. They deal with problems as they arise. But even for the experienced sailor fear can suddenly arrive, as it does with anyone else, to twist and pull the stomach as the seas rear and the wind starts its mournful whistling in the rigging.

Life without danger is dull, and all ocean sailors know that they are taking risks when they put to sea. The aim is to reduce the risk so that the fear level is kept under control and then everyone can enjoy the passage. For prospective transatlantic sailors this occurs if they have had a good deal of experience in their home waters before they set out. They go to the Caribbean because they want to voyage beyond the well-known line of their normal sea horizon. Reality will match the dream if their yacht is strong and seaworthy, if they have sailed through a storm before they set out to cross an ocean, if they have thought their way through a series of possible crises, if they have read widely, if the crew have sailed long and hard together and if the skipper has no doubt about his or her ability to navigate and use a sextant.

The dream also becomes a reality if the boat is well prepared and equipped for the tropics before it leaves its home port.

The equipment

Once in the Caribbean spares are expensive and difficult to obtain, so bring as many as you can with you. Charts for all the places you are likely to visit should be bought before you set out (a list is included at the end of the section on each country). British Admiralty charts are as good as any; indeed many other charts are based on them. But remember that many of these British charts were compiled over a hundred years ago and coral reefs continue to grow!

Very important pieces of equipment for the tropics are effective awnings - a small easily dowsed one for use on passage and a large (the larger the better) semi-permanent awning for use when at anchor. Make sure they are both designed to stay up in strong winds, at least Force 6, without flapping themselves to shreds. Despite the frequent tropical downpours it is often difficult to obtain supplies of fresh water, so a modification of the large awning to enable it to collect fresh water and deliver it to the yacht's tanks is a useful addition. Sail covers that are easy to fit are very important too as the tropical sunlight plays havoc with sail material. Always cover the sails as soon as you arrive at an anchorage - that way you will significantly prolong the life of your sails.

In the tropics ventilation is extremely important both above and below deck, and Dorade boxes with large, rotatable cowlings are a must. Ideally the fore hatch should open in two directions, but if you cannot afford one of these hatches rig up a wind chute to funnel air down into the accommodation. For safety reasons most British yachts have their fore hatches hinged forward in the belief that water breaking on the fore deck forces the hatch shut, but there are others which are hinged aft to act as wind scoops.

Other important pieces of equipment for an easy life when travelling in this region are a sturdy anchor winch, a readily accessible stern anchor and an easily available stern line to act as an anchor or stern warp - a line coiled on a drum that can easily be run out is a good idea. The anchorages described in this guide are sometimes subject to swells that can cause yachts to roll uncomfortably, so a stern anchor holding the bow onto the swell will considerably reduce the unpleasant roll.

Install a permanently mounted, strongly-built, metal bathing ladder in the stern. For the bunks, install stout lee cloths - for when crossing the Atlantic the sea will roll you out of your bed if you forget them. Also before you leave your home port purchase some very strong, UV-resistant plastic water containers. To be readily available they should be carried on deck as emergency water supplies and they will also act as a source of fresh water for showers. Canvas covers for these water containers will protect the plastic from the sun and give them a longer life. A black plastic shower bag, either home made or purchased cheaply in the Caribbean, can be hung off the backstay and is a simple way of warming water for that refreshing shower at the end of a hot day.

Keep the yacht's rig simple and strong. Make sure you carry light weather sails - the trade winds can often drop in mid-passage - and that you are able to reef the main (and the jib) quickly. Forty knot squalls are a feature of Caribbean island sailing and you need to reef fast (or else run off) as the towering black clouds and grey shafts of rain approach - unfortunately there is no way of knowing how much wind each squall will bring. Always carry a spare longest stay complete with a number of spare brass grommets for the Norseman terminals, if you use them, and a spare bottlescrew.

Most yachts use propane (Calor) gas for cooking and the bottles are easily replenished in the Caribbean (Camping Gaz is sometimes hard to find). A few diehards like myself continue to use paraffin - alcohol is readily available on the French islands for preheating the burners and it is never a problem to obtain paraffin. Many yachts carry ice boxes and providing they are well insulated ice blocks can be kept for at least 10 days. But ice is often hard to find in the Caribbean and it is expensive, so nowadays many yachts carry small electrically operated refrigerators. Modern wind generators or solar panels are able to supply enough current so there is no need to flatten the ship's batteries or continuously run the inboard motor. Most Caribbean yachts carry a wind generator mounted on a strong pole in the stern or directly on the mast, and increasingly solar panels are used - either permanently mounted or rigged when the yacht is at anchor.

Once you have set out across the Atlantic for the Caribbean you cannot turn back; you will be alone on a very large sea. Then for the dream to match reality you should aim to develop a harmonious relationship between a trustworthy yacht, the crew, the daily work and the aims of the voyage. The skipper should never push the boat, the people or the passage objectives too far; after all one of the main points of voyaging is to obtain maximum fulfilment and pleasure.

The landfall

The Caribbean hurricane season lasts from July to November, so yachts should aim to arrive in the islands before or after these months. The most popular time to cross the Atlantic is around the beginning of December, with the aim of spending Christmas in one of the Caribbean islands - Bequia is becoming increasingly popular if you like a crowd. The most favoured landfall with British yachts is, once again, Barbados - it became unpopular for a number of years because of the red tape and the cost of entering but this has now improved. However, an increasing number of yachts miss out Barbados and head straight for the excellent marina off Rodney Bay in north west Saint Lucia. Do remember though, that if you decide to miss out Barbados you will have a difficult beat against the trade winds if, at a later date, you wish to sail there from any of the other islands.

There are other possible landfalls. Some yachts sail directly to Martinique and the anchorage off Fort de France, identifying Cape Marquis on the north east coast of Saint Lucia at night, and Diamond Rock in the passage between Martinique and Saint Lucia, by day. Especially popular with French yachts is the superb marina at Pointe à Pitre, Guadeloupe. Yachts approaching Guadeloupe generally make a landfall on either the island of La Desirade or Petite Terre Island. A once popular landfall was the south coast of Antigua, but nowadays the light on Shirley Heights is not very reliable and the entrance to English Harbour is not easy if it is your first time. If you do decide to head for Antigua make a landfall on La Desirade or Petite Terre off Guadeloupe and then head north, allowing for one or two knots of westerly-going current between Guadeloupe and Antigua. Do not make landfalls on the north east coast of Antigua as it is low-lying and dangerous, or on Montserrat, Barbuda or Dominica as there are neither powerful, reliable lights nor facilities.

Some yachts head for Grenada, making a landfall in the south of the island. The powerful light south of Morne Rouge Bay on the west coast of Grenada has an unusual characteristic and can be seen from a long way out at sea. Others make a landfall on the south east corner of Saint Lucia at Vieux Fort where there is a good light or on the south east corner of Saint Vincent, before heading for the anchorage at Bequia. I have also known yachts that arrived at Trinidad, but given the poor welcome they received from Customs and Immigration I would not consider this island after a long hard transatlantic voyage.

My landfall recommendation, in decreasing terms of preference, would be: Barbados, north Saint Lucia, Martinique, Guadeloupe, south Saint Lucia, Saint Vincent, Grenada, Antigua, Trinidad and Tobago.

The weather

There is little variation in temperature all the year round, ranging from the mid to high twenties Celsius. The tropical sun burns white and black skins even when it is overcast or cloudy, so come well equipped with water-resistant, total-block sun tan lotions (15+) if you burn easily. There are, broadly speaking, two main seasons - a wet and a dry one. The dry season is from February to June and the wet season from about mid July to November. It may not rain for days in the dry season but in the wet season it will usually rain every day, sometimes very heavily for a few hours, but normally there will be only a short, heavy shower once or twice a day. There might be the odd overcast day in the wet season, but there will still be many hours of hot sunshine and blue skies. The wet season is the time of year for the vicious 40 knot squalls.

The trade winds vary from 10 to 25 knots throughout the year. They tend to be from the north through to the east in the winter months, and less strong and from the south through to the east in the summer months. In the winter a number of anchorages become uncomfortable because of a northerly swell from the North Atlantic. In summer and winter the swell in the inter-island passages is usually around one to two metres, occasionally three metres, and visibility can vary from a hazy five miles to generally around 15 to 20 miles, exceptionally 40 miles. The tidal range is low and varies between 0.3 to 0.5 metres. There is never any fog but yacht decks and sails are sometimes covered in a fine orange dust, carried from the Sahara in Africa to the Caribbean by the trade winds.

The islands and anchorages are most crowded in the winter months, when the charterers are fleeing the wet and cold of northern Europe and America, but the best sailing is often in the spring when the northerly swells die down and there is no risk of a hurricane. To see the Caribbean at its quiet and sleepy best, visit in the late summer when many hotels are shut, the charter boats are laid up and the bays and anchorages are almost empty - for it is the hurricane season.

But there is no need to be too worried: in the last 30 years less than 20 hurricanes have come ashore in the whole of the Caribbean to cause serious damage. There are only some six hurricanes a year (five of these are in August and September) and the local radio stations should give you at least three days', warning before they arrive, which should allow ample time to find a hurricane hole.

In the late summer months listen regularly to the weather bulletins and listen out for 'tropical waves' and 'tropical depressions' as these weather systems often, but not always, grow into 'tropical storms' (sustained winds between 35 and 63 knots) and hurricanes (above 64 knots). As a general rule, the further east a depression starts in the Atlantic, the more likely it is to develop into a hurricane, and the stonger the winds will be when the hurricane arrives in the Caribbean. The winds travel anti-clockwise around a centre of a hurricane which generally moves westwards or north-westwards across the Atlantic. Often the hurricanes curve in a north-easterly direction once they arrive in the Caribbean. The centre usually moves at anything between 5 and 20 knots an hour, and if you are some 200 miles south of the centre the winds will be around Force 6. But be careful as there are no real rules and hurricanes can curve back on themselves, the winds can increase or drop, and the centres suddenly speed up or slow down. As the hurricanes curve northwards generally they lose their power and above a latitude of 40° N they are usually downgraded to depressions.

If you sail amongst the Caribbean islands in late summer, plan to be within three days' sail of one of the following hurricane holes:

Antigua: the bays off English Harbour, and Parham in the north.
Guadeloupe: the Rivière Salée and possibly the Blue Lagoon.
Martinique: Cohe du Lamentin Marina, Trois Islets or the Cul de Sac du Marin.
Saint Lucia: Rodney Bay lagoon and possibly Marigot Harbour
Carriacou: Tyrrel Bay lagoon.

Grenada: at a pinch, St George's lagoon; and much better Calviney Harbour or Port Egmont.

Because of the widespread damage done in recent years by Hurricanes David, Allen, Emily and Hugo, many cruising yachts are sailing to Venezuela during the summer months to be out of the hurricane zone.

People, places and environment

It is well to respect the people, the places and the environment. The Caribbean and Venezuelan people are often God fearing and conservative and do not take kindly to rich, noisy, drunken tourists. Nudity is often frowned upon on the beaches as is swimwear in the towns, supermarkets and shops. Avoid throwing anything over the side at any anchorage; take everything ashore and drop the plastic bags in proper waste disposal units. In the open air markets there is sometimes some bargaining of prices, and for long taxi rides and local tours - but go about it politely as it is not usual to bargain over prices. Be careful not to confuse Eastern Caribbean dollars (EC dollars) with US dollars as both are accepted currencies in the ex-British colonies. (At the bank one dollar EC equals about 2.67 dollars US). Respect the fishing and spearfishing regulations. Never buy out of season or undersized lobsters or turtles, and never throw plastic bags over the side as turtles apparently mistake them for jelly fish and they can choke themselves to death.

The charter scene

In the last 20 years there has been an explosion of chartering in the Caribbean, to such an extent that something like 80 per cent of the boats sailing the region described in this guide are charter boats (see Table 1 (pages 14-15) for a list of some of the larger, well-established companies). Most are 'bare-boat' charters which are the cheapest and where the skipper and friends hire the boat for a fixed period, but nearly all the major charter companies also offer skippered and hostessed boats. It is possible, for an extra fee, to have a 'one way' charter where the yacht is sailed to a destination and the charter company will pick it up and return it to base, but most charters are an 'out and back' arrangement. The charter yachts are usually fibreglass, in excellent condition and made in France or America. The usual range offered by the companies is from around 7.6 to 17 metres but of course there are some magnificent charter boats available for hire (Antigua is one of the best places in the Caribbean from which to hire superb, large boats). Because of the wind and seas in the inter-island passages it is best to hire a boat of around 12 metres, especially if you want reasonably fast, comfortable crossings.

Once you have arrived in the Caribbean it is possible to arrange day charters from most of the major hotels or at the marinas. You will be taken out by a skipper along with a number of other clients for a sail (usually a motor sail) to a local beauty spot for lunch, a swim and an evening cocktail. Otherwise book your charter holiday before you arrive in the islands. If you are chartering for a week or more and coming from Europe, and if you can afford it, I would strongly recommend that you spend a few days in a local hotel acclimatising yourself to the heat and recovering from jet-lag before you set out on your charter. You can charter a yacht singly, as a family or as a group. An individual, couple, family or group can, of course, join another charter group on a large yacht in much the same way as a passenger would join a cruise ship. Antigua, Guadeloupe, Martinique, Saint Lucia, Saint Vincent and Grenada all have very experienced charter companies and they all advertise in the yachting press. It is a good idea to check if bed linen, an outboard motor, a dinghy, snorkelling gear, a windsurfer, and a spinnaker are included in the price.

The hazards

Watch out for the sun! Many a charter has spoilt a Caribbean holiday by walking around on the boat without sun tan lotion and a T-shirt. Remember to use a total-block lotion if you burn easily - and always apply it liberally to those parts that stick out, like ears and nose. A cotton sun hat worn at all times during the day is an excellent idea.

There are almost no accounts of robberies and attacks by local people on visitors to the islands. As a precaution against theft always lock up the yacht when you leave it unattended, and when going ashore it pays to use wire strops and padlocks to secure the outboard to the dinghy and the dinghy to the dock.

There are no records of unprovoked attacks by sharks or barracuda in the Caribbean waters covered in this guide, but avoid swimming at night and becoming the first recorded casualty! There are, however, a number of drownings each year from swimming, sailing and windsurfing. The winds and currents are strong in the inter-island passages and the seas high, so keep to the sheltered bays on the leeward side of the islands. Black spiky sea urchins should not be handled or trodden on, but if you do, use a disinfectant and remove the protruding spikes with a pair of tweezers. Avoid scratching yourself on the coral as the graze will take a long time to heal, especially if you do not clean it well once you return to the yacht. If you are snorkelling for a long period, or over a coral reef, wear a T-shirt to protect your back against sunburn and your front against the sharp coral.

Ashore the worst danger is the Manchineel tree, which is common along the shores throughout the region. Do not eat its yellow to bright green, little apples which can produce terrible rashes and ulcers when handled or eaten, and avoid standing under the tree when it rains as the toxin can wash off. In Saint Lucia there is a nasty fresh water liver parasite living in some of streams, so do not swim in them. Most islands have no dangerous snakes except Saint Lucia and Martinique which have the rare Fer de Lance.

There is no malaria at present in the Caribbean. However, the mosquitoes are an incredible nuisance, especially if you anchor too close to the shore or in a windless anchorage. They can be kept at bay with mosquito coils and repellent, as can the almost invisible, viciously-biting sandflies that appear on the beaches at dusk and will ruin a barbecue for you if you have forgotten to take repellent. A species of Caribbean mosquito will pass on dengue and yellow fever. Yellow fever is absent in the islands but there have been recent outbreaks deep inside Venezuela. I know of a few isolated cases of dengue fever in the Caribbean which appears like a bad case of flu, with aches and pains in the joints. Be warned - a second dengue infection can be dangerous or even fatal.

No matter how hard you try to avoid it, you will from time to time get a cockroach infestation. To keep these to a minimum it is important to wash all fruit and vegetables thoroughly in a bucket of fresh or salt water and let them dry in the sun before taking them below. Never take cardboard cartons or egg containers from supermarkets on board, and inspect all plastic bags for cockroaches

A barracuda comes aboard off Saint Lucia

before you stow them away. Boric acid crystals (obtainable from any chemist) sprinkled around the inside of the boat work well in preventing a cockroach epidemic, and as for that extra large flying cockroach, you can down it with a squirt from any pesticide aerosol. Cockroaches may look horrible but they are essentially harmless.

When trolling for fish south of Martinique any small fish (under 2 kg) you catch is usually considered by the local fishermen to be safe to eat and free from ciguatera poisoning. Ciguatera poisoning is a nasty neurological complaint able to cause vomiting, diarrhoea, muscle pain, urine retention, headaches and tingling in the joints and limbs and needs immediate medical attention. The toxin is produced by a blue-green micro-algae that is said to inhabit damaged coral reefs. The toxin is accumulated in the alimentary tract of fish and is not destroyed by cooking. The toxin can be found in any fish. It is quite often found in large barracuda and king fish north of Martinique, so if you want to avoid it don't eat these fish north of Martinique.

A serious danger to cruising yachts is the Caribbean buoyage and lights system - or rather the lack of it. In theory since 1984 the islands have operated on the IALA System B and the Cardinal System. That is, red buoys on the starboard side and green buoys on the port side when entering a harbour (the 'red right returning' rule). It is fair to say that the French islands and the wealthiest ex-British colonies look after their buoys and lighthouses, but most countries do not. The buoys are usually unlit when they should be lit, sometimes missing, or worse, out of position, and sometimes with different characteristics from those marked on the charts. Few lighthouses work at their published ranges and some do not work at all. In short, the situation is so bad that most experienced skippers will not travel amongst the islands at night. You are asking for trouble if you stay close inshore. There are a few radiobeacons but they are for aeroplanes and are rarely used for inter-island navigation.

But it is wrong to end on the hazards. Sailing the Caribbean from Antigua to Venezuela is to travel in one of the world's finest cruising grounds: the warm steady winds are aft of the beam, the anchorages less than a day sail away, the sunshine is certain, the sea temperature is perfect for bathing, and the deep blue sky is lightly spattered with the tiny, puff-ball trade wind clouds - could anything be more delightful?

Table 1: Caribbean Charter Companies

Local charter Companies	European/North American Addresses	Comments
ANTIGUA		
Nicholson's Yacht Charter Nelson's Dockyard, English Harbour Tel: 463 1530	432 Columbia St, Cambridge MA, USA. Tel: 800 662 6066 or 617 225 0555	Long established charter company. Luxury skippered yachts a speciality. All charter possibilities.
Seagull Yachts Nelson's Dockyard Post Office, English Harbour Tel: 463 1738	PO Box 737, Camden, Maine, USA. Tel: 800 772 3500/ 207	Skippered and bareboats.
Sun Yachts PO Box 271, St John's Tel: 463 2115		Skippered and bareboats.
GRENADA		
Go Vacations Box 308, St George's Tel: 444 4257	Offices in Canada. Tel: Toronto 674 1880 or 800 387 3996	
The Moorings Hartman Bay, Secret Harbour, PO Box 11, St George's Tel: 444 4548		New venture by The Moorings charter company.
GUADELOUPE		
ATM Place Creole, Gosier Tel: 90 9202		Large charter organisation with its major base in Martinique (see p15). Skippered, bareboat and one way charters.
Blue Caraibe/Tropical Yacht Services Marina du Bas du Fort, Pointe à Pitre Tel: 90 8060		
Soleil et Voile Marina du Bas du Fort, Pointe à Pitre Tel: 90 8181		Multihulls a speciality
Vacances Yachting Marina du Bas du Fort, Pointe à Pitre Tel: 90 8295		Bareboats, one way charters, monohulls and multihulls.

Table 1(contd): Caribbean Charter Companies

Local Charter Companies	European/North American Addresses	Comments
MARTINIQUE		
ATM Club Nautique, Le Marin Tel: 749 817/8788	8 Rue Sédillot, Paris 75007, France. Tel: 470 56386	One of the largest charter fleets in the Caribbean offering all possibilities.
Chimère/Tropic Yachting Marina de la Pointe du Bout, Trois Ilets Tel: 660 385	20 Rue Victor Bart, Versailles, France.	Bareboats, one ways, monohulls and multihulls.
Soleil et Voile Marina de la Pointe du Bout Tel: 660 914		Also based in Guadeloupe.
Star Voyage Antilles Marina de la Pointe du Bout Tel: 660 072	5 Rue Lincoln, Paris 75008, France. Tel: 425 61562	Skippered, bareboat and one way charter.
St LUCIA		
Stevens Yachts PO Box 928, Rodney Bay Marina Tel: 28648	50 Water St, South Norwalk, CT USA. Tel: 800 45 28848/28648	Long established American charter company offering all possibilities.
Trade Wind Charter Rodney Bay Marina Tel: 28424	778 Wimborne Rd, Bournemouth, UK. Tel: 0202 5201.	An Anglo American co also with offices in New York.Tel: 800 222 6656.
The Moorings PO Box 101, Marigot Bay Tel: 34246/34256	The Moorings, Suite 402, 19 South St, Clearwater FA 33546, USA.Tel: 800 535 7289	Internationally famous American charter company.
St VINCENT		
CSY PO Box 133, Blue Lagoon Tel: 84308/908	Box 491, Tenafly, NJ 0760, USA. Tel: 800 631 1593	Long established American charter company.
Bimini Yacht Vacations PO Box 39, Blue Lagoon Tel: 69324	431 Richmond St East, Toronto, Canada. Tel: 416 366 1777	No one-ways.

BARBADOS

It is probable that Barbados was first inhabited by South American Barrancoid Indians who arrived on Barbados around the time of the birth of Christ. Around 800 AD they were replaced by the Arawaks who, some 400 years later, were either killed or enslaved by the Caribs. The Spanish were the next to arrive and they either killed the Caribs or shipped them out to work as slaves in Hispaniola. When a Portuguese expedition led by Pedro a Campos landed on Barbados in 1536 it found an uninhabited island. Campos named the island Los Barbados - the bearded ones - after the struggling fig trees that grew along the shoreline. The Portuguese decided that Los Barbados was not worth colonising, as did the French and the Dutch who were the next Europeans to arrive. But an English sea captain, stumbling on Barbados in 1625 as a result of a navigational error, believed he could make his fortune by growing tobacco on the island's lowlands. He claimed Barbados for England and returned two years later with 80 settlers and 10 slaves (taken as a prize from a captured Portuguese ship) and landed at Holetown. Sailors later named this first settlement Holetown after shallow Limehouse Hole on the River Thames.

In 1628 other British settlers landed south of Holetown and, finding a derelict Amerindian bridge near their landing site, named their settlement Bridgetown. Barbados prospered, and within 10 years over 2000 British colonists were profitably exporting tobacco, indigo and cotton. In 1637 sugar cane was brought to Barbados and it quickly replaced all the other crops. But sugar production required large numbers of workers, and the supply of white indentured labour from Britain - often criminals escaping the gallows - was never sufficient to meet an ever-increasing European demand for sugar.

Large numbers of African slaves were shipped to Barbados, and by the end of the century some 40 000 black slaves were owned by less than 1000 whites.

By the end of the seventeenth century a Barbados Parliament existed, but power rested firmly in the hands of the white plantation owners where it remained for centuries. From time to time the indentured white servants or the plantation slaves rebelled, but the uprisings were quickly and cruelly suppressed. The island was almost unaffected by the centuries of Anglo-French conflict in the Caribbean. Located some 100 miles to windward of the French bases in Martinique, it was difficult for the French square-rigged warships to beat against the trade winds - whenever the French fleets set out to attack Barbados the strong winds scattered them and sent them back.

The African slaves were freed in 1834, and by the end of the nineteenth century the Barbados Parliament was accepting non-white members. In 1966 Barbados became fully independent, but the effects of hundreds of years of uninterrupted British colonial rule are still much in evidence: the language, the structure of government, the official uniforms and the colonial architecture all reflect British influence. Sugar production declined after World War I and tourism became, and continues to be, very important for the island's economy. Barbados is naturally beautiful - the coral reefs, steep sea cliffs and wild crashing breakers of the windward side differ markedly from the golden sanded beaches and calm turquoise seas of the leeward coast to the west.

Today, in comparison with many other Caribbean islands, Barbados is wealthy. It has been extensively but imaginatively developed - especially along the leeward coast - and just recently offshore oil and gas deposits have been discovered. The population is around 250 000.

Yachting in Barbados has had a chequered history. Few yachts attempt the 100 mile or so upwind slog to Barbados from Martinique or Saint Lucia, although for years Barbados was the first stop for yachts crossing the Atlantic from east to west. However, when a deep water port was built at the island's capital, Bridgetown, entering and clearing became a long, expensive, paper filled drudge. Transatlantic British yachts began to bypass Barbados and head for English Harbour, Antigua, and French yachts went straight to the marinas in Martinique and Guadeloupe. Barbados has now made the entrance formalities easier and cheaper, and the island's popularity with transatlantic yachts is returning. Recent Atlantic Cruising Rallies (the ARC) have terminated in Barbados and in order to improve yachting facilities the government is considering building a marina. This would be much appreciated as the anchorage in Barbados is in huge and open Carlisle Bay in the south west corner of the island. Although Carlisle Bay is well sheltered, Atlantic swells can enter and make the anchorage uncomfortable; also there is only one landing dock.

Carlisle Bay

Approach
From the Atlantic the aim is to arrive off the east coast of Barbados just before dawn, when the glare of the island's house and street lights will be seen long before the flashing light of Ragged Point lighthouse (Fl 15s 213ft 21M). Other good landmarks are the red lights of the radio mast on Mount Misery, which is situated more or less in the centre of the island, and in the south of the island the lights of Seawell airport. The airport has a useful and powerful radiobeacon (BGI, 345 kHz, 1.2 kW).

Off the south west coast of Barbados there is South Point light (Gp Fl(3) 20s 145ft 17M) whose range is three miles less than Ragged Point light. Do not approach the island's south east coast too closely because south from Ragged Point to South Point there are reefs that extend 1½ miles offshore. Needham Point has a sectored light (Fl (4) WR 25s 43ft 14/10M). The white sector is the safe sector and the red sector shines over the reefs that extend both north and south of the point.

Once past Needham Point, call Barbados Harbour Control on VHF ch 16 or 26 to obtain permission to enter the deep water harbour, easily identified by the tall loading towers on its west wall. Approach the harbour and when you see the entrance, turn to starboard (the end of the west wall has a light, Gp Fl (3) 10s 46ft 12M) and steer for the customs quay which is at the southern head of the main basin. Go alongside, deal with the authorities, and then head out for the anchorage in Carlisle Bay.

From the Caribbean make a landfall on the north west of the island at Harrison Point which has a light (Gp Fl (2) 15s 193ft 20M). The best approach is from Martinique in the winter months, when you might be lucky to make Barbados on one long port tack. In the summer months when the winds are lighter and more southerly it might be possible to sail to Barbados from Tobago or Grenada on the starboard tack.

Half a mile offshore clears all dangers on the west coast of Barbados except for Kettle Bottom and Pelican Shoals, which are situated about a mile north of the entrance to the deep water harbour.

Anchorage

Most visiting yachts anchor off the Boatyard dock in Carlisle Bay. The Boatyard bar/restaurant has become the unofficial centre of yachting in Barbados, and is situated about a quarter of a mile south east of the entrance to the Carenage. Drop your anchor into good holding sand in depths of between 6 to 10 metres a little way off the Boatyard jetty. Yachts can anchor almost anywhere in Carlisle Bay, from the oil tanker jetty just south of the west harbour wall round to the pier off the Royal Barbados Yacht Club, but the Boatyard has the only dock.

Ashore

The Boatyard's bar and restaurant are at the head of the dock and it is safe to leave the dinghy here. The management of the Boatyard is very helpful, and ice, laundry and fresh water showers are available. Fuel and water can be loaded from the end of the dock (there is also a fuelling dock inside the deep water harbour). If you wish to haul out, the Boatyard will organise a lift out in the deep water harbour for yachts displacing up to 25 tons, and long-term dry storage can be arranged - but be careful to remove all valuables from the boat as there have been some break-ins. Broken booms, bent masts, ripped sails, smashed stanchions and faulty engines can all be repaired, as the Boatyard has a contact list of riggers, sailmakers, aluminium and stainless steel welders and reliable diesel mechanics - even new masts can be obtained.

From the Boatyard Bridgetown is easily accessible on foot. In or near the town there are supermarkets, bars and restaurants, night clubs, hotels, underwater diving parks, wildlife reserves, rum distilleries, a post office, a cricket ground, and a race track - in fact everything except a first class yacht chandlery. The Carenage is an interesting place to visit, to drink a beer, or have a meal and watch the Barbadian fishing craft and day charter yachts. There is a public quay on the north bank of the Carenage but it is always crowded.

The Royal Barbados Yacht Club opens its facilities to visiting

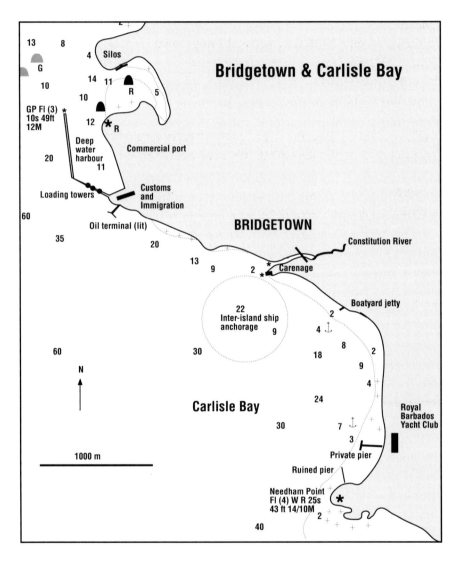

members of bona fide yacht clubs and the Holiday Inn is a centre for scuba diving. Barbados has an international airport at Seawell with regular flights to London and New York.

Customs and Immigration

Both are situated in the large building at the head of the main quay in the deep water harbour, and officials are there from 0600 to 2200 hours. The total entrance (and clearing) fee is around $25 US. Yachts arriving outside these hours should anchor off in Carlisle Bay and hoist the Q flag. Next morning call the authorities on VHF ch 16 prior to entering the deep water harbour.

Charts
British Admiralty: 2485 General, 502 Bridgetown
French: 3200 General
USA: 25485 General
Imray Iolaire: B2 General

Radio Stations, Frequency and Times of Weather Bulletin
Radio Barbados: 900 kHz (0718, 0802,1430,1843)

Airport
International airport in the south of the island.

ANTIGUA

At the time of Columbus' first voyage to the West Indies in 1492 most of the Caribbean islands were already inhabited by either the Arawak or Carib Indians, tribes that had migrated north from South America. The gentle Arawak Indians were the first to arrive in the islands, travelling north from the Orinoco basin through Trinidad and Grenada from around the first century AD to about 1200. When Columbus arrived in 1492 the Arawaks were gradually being exterminated by fiercer Amerindians, the cannibalistic Caribs, who probably arrived in the islands around 1000 AD. The Caribs killed the Arawak males and enslaved the Arawak women. As these Arawak women continued to speak their own language Europeans at first believed that the island natives had two languages - one for men and another for women. Much has been made of the cannibalism of the Caribs but, while it is certain that the Caribs ate human flesh, it is unlikely that it was their main diet; probably they only ritualistically ate enemy warriors so as to take their powers. Columbus, mistakenly believing he had arrived in Asia, thought that the Caribs were soldiers fighting for the Chinese Emperor Kubla Khan. Columbus saw but did not land on Antigua during his second voyage to the West Indies in 1493. He named the island after a painting of the Virgin Mary - Santa Maria la Antigua - that was in Seville Cathedral.

Columbus left his discoveries in Central and South America to Spain, his paymaster. Hungry for gold the Spanish conquered, plundered and ransacked the advanced American civilisations and, easily subduing the remaining Arawak tribes, set up colonies in the larger Caribbean islands of Cuba, Jamaica and Hispaniola (Haiti and Santo Domingo). Spain left the smaller Caribbean islands populated by the fiercer Carib Indians to France, the next colonial power to arrive in the islands. The French colonists massacred the Caribs whenever there were outbreaks of aggression, and colonised Guadeloupe, Dominica, Martinique, St Lucia and Grenada. English colonists were the next to arrive and claimed what France and Spain had left - isolated Barbados, tiny Montserrat and, in 1632, dry (because of the lack of high mountains) Antigua.

By the seventeenth century Europeans were becoming addicted to the recently discovered drinks - coffee and tea. These beverages were ideally sweetened with sugar that was replacing honey as the traditional sweetener. Soon the European markets were clamouring for sugar in ever increasing amounts. The West Indies' sugar cane, the European planters and their African slaves supplied the need. It was a lucrative trade and sugar became the drive that made the Caribbean a battleground for some three hundred years. The competing empire building nations - Spain, France, Holland and England - fought for control of the cane fields, and all the Caribbean islands changed hands at least once.

By the mid to late eighteenth century England had become a powerful nation and had made many conquests. In order to consolidate its position two important and permanent West Indian naval bases were established, one at Port Royal in Jamaica and the other at English Harbour in Antigua. (England's main rival, France, sent her naval ships back to Europe each year to refit and avoid the hurricane season). Although throughout the Caribbean there are many relics of the long wars between France and England, today the British navy has long departed. English Harbour on the shores of a flooded volcano cone, abandoned as a naval base, still remains a sheltered haven and has become a classical yacht anchorage and a centre of tourism. English Harbour dockyard was recently restored to some of its former glory and today the area is a national park.

Antigua and Barbuda became independent in 1981, and now tourism has replaced sugar as the island's main industry. The capital of the two-island nation is St John's, situated in the north west of Antigua at the head of a large bay, St John's Harbour. This is a good deep-water harbour but is more suited to cargo ships than yachts. There are, however, over a dozen superb yacht anchorages around the coasts of Antigua (and more around Barbuda) all less than a day's sail apart. Most yachts arriving in Antigua for the first time head for the southern part of the island and English Harbour.

English Harbour

The anchorage in Freeman Bay, the first bay of English Harbour, is one of the great Caribbean anchorages - beautiful, breezy and safe. Connected to Freeman Bay are even two hurricane holes, one in Ordnance Bay and the other in Tank Bay.

Approach

The entrance to English Harbour is notoriously difficult to find for the first time. When approaching *from Guadeloupe or Montserrat* the 'views' drawn in the *British Admiralty West Indies Pilot (Vol II)* are excellent (see page 350, 1969 ed). Great George and Dow Hill forts do not nowadays make good landmarks as they are broken down and overgrown with vegetation. The tall mast light on Cape Shirley (Fl (4) 20s, 494ft high with a range of 20 miles) will assist in the identification of the prominent flat-topped hills of Shirley Heights. The westernmost ruin on Shirley Heights overlooks English Harbour. The crenellations of the partially restored Fort Barclay are very distinctive and mark the west side of the entrance into English Harbour. Just south of the east side of this entrance, which is reef-strewn Charlotte Point, there are some conspicuous column-shaped rocks aptly known as the 'Pillars of Hercules'. When approaching English Harbour *from either a southerly or westerly direction* keep clear of the reefs off Johnson Point and the unmarked Middle and Cade reefs. When approaching Antigua *from an easterly direction* give the dangerous north east coast of the island a wide berth as it is very low lying and full of unmarked reefs.

Through the entrance in to Freeman Bay there is a depth of over 7 metres of water but make sure you give the reef off Charlotte Point a good clearance. The harbour is best entered by day, but if for any reason you have to enter at night (and I would not recommend this for your first approach to the harbour) as you come through the entrance you might be lucky enough to spot the two red leading lights that are rigged on telegraph poles on the shore of Freeman Bay - the lower light (Qk Fl R) suspended at 10.7 metres and the upper (Iso R 2s) at 25.9 metres. The lights are not very powerful and the lower light can sometimes be obscured by the masts of anchored yachts.

Anchorage

Drop anchor in good holding sand in 3 to 7 metres of water anywhere in gently-shelving Freeman Bay. Leave a clear passage through to the

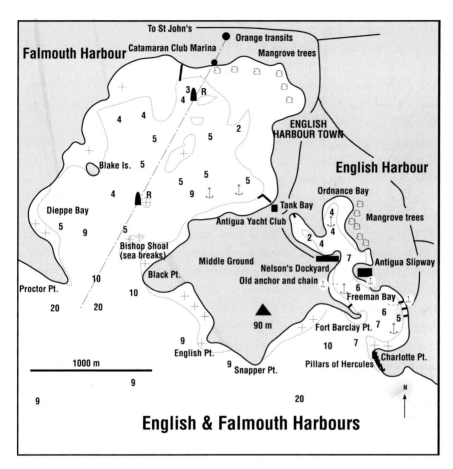

English & Falmouth Harbours

Nelson's Dockyard quays, the Antigua Slipway docks and the anchorages in Tank and Ordnance Bays.

It is possible to moor stern-to on the quays at Nelson's Dockyard where there is some 4 metres of water. Bow anchors have to be dropped nearly as far over as the Antigua Slipway docks, or the mangrove trees for the inner quay of Nelson's Dockyard, since the holding in the middle of the through passage is poor. Yachts also moor stern-to at the Antigua Slipway berths opposite Nelson's Dockyard. Electricity and water are available at the berths.

Four large hurricane chains were laid across English Harbour by the British Navy in the days of sail, and the massive cast iron holding anchor on the beach in the middle of Freeman Bay is clearly visible when you enter the bay for the first time. The hurricane chains not only acted as strong mooring chains, but they were also grappled by incoming ships to slow themselves down - rather like the arrester wire on an aircraft carrier. Avoid dropping your anchor on these chains.

Alongside and Ashore

English Harbour naval base was completed around the middle of the eighteenth century. In 1784 Horatio Nelson arrived, and during his three-year posting eventually became commander-in-chief of the base and of all the Leeward Islands. Nelson briefly visited English Harbour in 1805 to water his ships before continuing his transatlantic chase of Admiral Villeneuve that finally led to the defeat of the French Navy at the battle of Trafalgar. Today English Harbour Dockyard has been restored, and to commemorate its links with Britain's most famous Admiral it is known as Nelson's Dockyard. In 1985 the Dockyard became a National Park.

Within Nelson's Dockyard is a bakery, a sail maker, a marine electronics repair shop, a mechanical engineer, a rigging specialist, a first class hotel, bars, restaurants and boutiques, showers and do-it-yourself laundry facilities behind A&F Sails (take along a wooden bung as a plug), a bank, a post office and telephones for local and international calls (reverse the charges if you can; it is much easier). Just outside the Dockyard is the Carib Marine, a well-stocked supermarket and chandlery.

The enchanting little Dockyard museum contains Nelson memorabilia and the 30 gleaming trophies awarded to the winning yachts that take part in the annual Antigua Sailing Week. This event was started in 1927 when a number of local charter yacht skippers decided to blow off steam at the end of the charter season by participating in a race to decide who had the fastest charter boat. The idea took off and today Antigua Sailing Week has become a major offshore ocean racing event. Yachts from all over the world come to compete in the five races that take place during the last week in April. In early December the Charter Agents Show takes place at Nelson's Dockyard, where you might be able to find a job or put your boat up for charter.

Opposite Nelson's Dockyard is the Antigua Slipway which can haul yachts up to 125 tons displacement. It has an efficient hydraulic trailer that can lift smaller yachts displacing up to 25 tons. The management of Antigua Slipway does not allow owners to work on their own boats - local labour has to be used, and the yard publishes a rate card for the prices of most jobs. Beware of the rider 'bottoms in poor condition may cost more to prepare for painting'. There is a diesel and fresh water dock at the Antigua Slipway and a large, fairly expensive chandlery.

English and Falmouth Harbours from Shirley Heights

There are plenty of things to do and see in and around English Harbour. The Dockyard has the quiet, sophisticated Admiral's Inn and the beautifully restored hotel, bar and restaurant at the Copper and Lumber Store. There are dive shops offering shallow and deep water scuba dives. Outside the dockyard, just off Freeman Bay beach, is an Italian restaurant, Colombo's, which has a band on Wednesday and Friday nights. The Inn restaurant, a short hike up the hill from the beach, offers candlelight dining on its terrace. A visit to the Lookout bar and restaurant at the top of Shirley Heights is a must on a Sunday afternoon and evening when there is a barbecue and a steel band. The climb up to Shirley Heights from Freeman Bay gives fine views of English and Falmouth Harbours, and the top is a wonderful place from which to contemplate the setting sun.

Most yacht-related businesses continuously monitor VHF channel 68 in English Harbour and 'English Harbour Radio' is manned by Nicholson's Yacht Charter and Travel Services on SSB 4124 MHz as well as VHF ch 68. Every morning at 0900 Jolyon Byerley comes on English Harbour Radio, ch 68, to remind everyone to turn to ch 6 where he gives a 24-hour weather forecast. It is also possible to obtain an excellent daily and long term weather forecast by telephoning the meteorological office at VC Bird international airport any time night or day on 462 3017 or 462 0930 (see also page 33).

Buses run regularly to St John's, and although the fare is cheap the ride takes over an hour. Taxis can be obtained outside the Dockyard but they are expensive.

Customs and Immigration

Once at anchor in Freeman Bay yachts should hoist the Q flag. The skipper then takes the ship's papers to the customs and immigration office in Nelson's Dockyard and then, if staying at anchor in English Harbour, has to register the yacht with the National Parks Authority.

Out of season (during the summer and autumn months) the immigration office is situated in the police building outside the Dockyard. Yachts are charged for anchoring in English Harbour ($0.15 US per foot per week, but note that anchoring is free in Falmouth Harbour from 1 June to 30 November). Yachts have to pay a Dockyard entry fee of $5 US. There is also a port entry fee, and skippers must obtain a cruising permit for Antigua and Barbuda. Both are priced according to the yacht's length - for example, for a yacht between 41 to 81 ft, the port entry fee is $6 US and the monthly cruising permit is $10 US. Customs and immigration offices are open from 0600 to 1800 every day of the year and there are no overtime charges.

Falmouth Harbour

Close to English Harbour is the other famous classical anchorage in southern Antigua, Falmouth Harbour. This is a large, sheltered, all weather harbour (except in hurricanes) whose entrance is situated some two miles west of English Harbour. Although the water is less clear than in Freeman Bay, and not as pleasant for bathing, Falmouth Harbour is larger and breezier than English Harbour and tends to be the preferred anchorage of longer-staying cruising yachts.

Approach

The entrance to Falmouth Harbour is easy by day, but should not be attempted by night as the leading lights rarely work and there are dangerous unlit shoals especially inside the entrance. As you approach the entrance during daytime look out for the sea breaking over unmarked Bishop Shoal which lies just north of Black Point, the east entrance to Falmouth Harbour. Proctor or Gualdin Point, the west side of the entrance, is reasonably steep-to. After clearing Bishop

Shoal, yachts can either turn to starboard and head for the anchorage off the new dock by the Antigua Yacht Club, or head for about a mile in a northerly direction to the Catamaran Club Marina at the head of the harbour.

There is a buoyed reef in the middle of Falmouth Harbour which needs to be avoided when heading north for the Catamaran Club Marina. You will have a safe passage by lining up the two orange triangles and approaching the marina on this transit, leaving the red buoys to starboard. At night there are two green leading lights that, if lit, will guide you to the Catamaran Club Marina: the front lower light (Qk Fl G) is suspended at 10.6 metres and the rear (Iso G 2s) at 22.8 metres.

Anchorage
Yachts can anchor almost anywhere in Falmouth Harbour in good holding sand in depths of 3 to 7 metres providing they keep clear of the centre reef and the shoals and rocks around Blake Island.

Alongside and Ashore
The Catamaran Club Marina has 30 berths (maximum 4.25 metres draft), diesel, water, ice, telephones and a restaurant. The anchorage off the Antigua Yacht Club is close to the Port Authority's fuelling and water dock, and the well stocked shelves of the Carib Marine supermarket and the delights of Nelson's Dockyard are not far away.

Customs and Immigration
Yachts should first enter Antigua at English Harbour and then proceed to Falmouth Harbour.

Crabbs Marina

Crabbs Marina in Parham Harbour on the north east coast of Antigua is another classical Antiguan anchorage. The north east coast of Antigua is very low-lying and extremely dangerous and Crabbs Marina should only be approached from the west or north coasts of Antigua. Crabbs Marina is situated in Parham Harbour and off the marina there is a safe and comfortable anchorage. Crabbs Marina is an excellent boatyard that is within easy reach of the island's capital and Antigua's international airport.

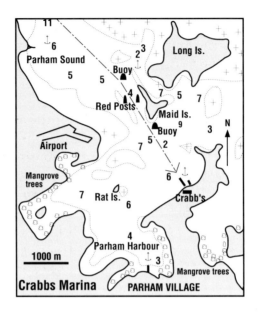

Approach

This is best from the west end of Boon Channel. Travel through Boon Channel during the day, ideally with the sunlight high and behind you so that dangerous Diamond Bank and Horse Shoe reefs can be identified. There is a conspicuous tower on the west end of Diamond Bank which is to the north of the western entrance to Boon Channel. Prickly Pear Island, located near the eastern end of the channel, is surrounded by reefs and most local yachtsmen prefer to pass between Prickly Pear Island and the mainland. Sail fairly close to the shore in Parham Sound and keep away from the reefs that stretch away to the north west of Long Island. The dredged channel into Parham Harbour is about 5 metres deep and is marked, at the time of writing, by a faded, large red buoy at the north east of Maid Island and another faded red buoy at the south of the island. Leave both these buoys to port - against the normal 'red right returning' convention - but this may be corrected by the time this guide goes to print so take care. Pass between the two red posts that are about halfway along the island. Once past the buoy at the south end of Maid Island, Crabbs Marina and the anchorage are up ahead.

Anchorage

Steer directly for the marina and anchor in 3 to 4 metres of water. There are two anchorages on the approach to Parham Harbour, one in Jumby Bay off the west coast of Long Island and the other off the west coast of Maid Island near the two red posts. The south part of Parham

Harbour, off the town of Parham, makes a good hurricane hole. Yachts tie up to the mangroves and drop their anchors in a depth of 3 metres into black sticky mud.

Alongside and Ashore
Crabbs Marina has space for some 50 yachts, and yachts can also be dry stored ashore at reasonable rates. There is diesel, electricity and ice and a good cooling breeze. The yard has a 50 ton travel lift and owners can work on their boats. There is a chandlery, telephones, laundry, restaurant, showers and a post office. The yard is not situated at a very scenic part of the coast but the facilities are good and it is clean. The nearby village of Parham, which has a restaurant and a supermarket, is worth a visit as it used to be the home of the Governor of Antigua. Nowadays it is a quiet little backwater.

Customs and Immigration
If entering Antigua, the skipper should hoist the Q flag and report to the customs and immigration office which is opposite the chandlery in Crabbs Marina. The office is open from 0830 to 1630.

Almost all the anchorages in Antigua could be described as classical, and I have concentrated on the most popular. But there are others:

Indian Creek

This anchorage is situated about 2 miles east of English Harbour and is an excellent hurricane hole. There is about 3 metres of water a quarter of a mile in, and a thick mangrove swamp to tie up to. When entering the Creek watch out for Sunken Rock that lies just below the surface at the entrance - the sea usually breaks there.

Mamora Bay

This anchorage is about a quarter of a mile east of Indian Creek. An exclusive yacht club/marina, the St James Yacht Club, has been built on the east side of the lagoon and provides all manner of services for the visiting yacht, from horse riding and water skiing to tennis and croquet - providing you first pay a membership fee. There is a 38-berth marina with electricity, ice, water and fuel. The entrance to Mamora Bay is through a well buoyed channel. Enter the bay and leave the red buoys on the starboard bow and the green buoys on the port bow. The inner lagoon has around 3 metres depth of water and a muddy bottom and you can anchor anywhere, but most yachts choose to anchor off the St James Yacht Club.

Green Island and Nonsuch Bay

From English Harbour Green Island is about a 9-mile upwind slog against the trade winds and Atlantic swell. A white house on Friar's Head is a good landmark. Leave York Island to port (steer about 313° Magnetic) and keep Green Island on the starboard bow. Beware of Submarine Rock on the port bow and anchor in Rickett Harbour at the west end of Green Island. The smaller anchorage on the east of the island at Tenpond Bay can only take a couple of yachts. From Rickett Harbour if you have had some experience at reef navigation you can pass into delightful, calm, deep Nonsuch Bay. Green Island is owned by the Mill Reef Club but you are allowed ashore.

Deep Bay

This is one of the best anchorages on the west coast of Antigua and situated just south of the entrance to St John's Harbour, the island's capital. When approaching the anchorage from the west look out for Sandy Island and Weymouth Reef some three miles offshore. In the middle of Deep Bay is the conspicuous wreck of the *Andes*; pass it on either side and anchor in sand in 3 metres of water off the Royal Antiguan Hotel.

Five Island Harbour

Situated about three miles south of Deep Bay, you should give the Barrel of Beef Rocks a wide margin and enter the Harbour to anchor west of, and close to, Maid Island in about 4 metres depth of water. There is also an anchorage off Stony Horn in about 5 metres of water.

There are other daytime and overnight anchorages around the coast of Antigua, and of course there is **Barbuda** which lies some 30 miles north of Antigua. Some cruising people believe Barbuda is the most beautiful of all the Caribbean islands. But navigating a yacht around Barbuda is difficult - there are many uncharted reefs and coral heads - and some experience in navigating 'by eye' through reefs is essential before you attempt the 30 mile trip.

Charts
British Admiralty: 2064 General with details of English and Falmouth Harbours, 2065 North coast and St John's
USA: 25570 General and English Harbour, 25575 St John's to Parham
Imray Iolaire: A27 General, A271 North coast

Radio Station, Frequency and Times of Weather Bulletin
ABBS: 630 kHz
ZDK: 1100 kHz
VHF 68: 0900

International Airport
VC Bird international airport is situated about 20 minutes taxi ride away from the capital of Antigua, St John's. Tel: 462 3017 or 462 0930

MONTSERRAT

Montserrat was sighted by Columbus in 1493 during his second voyage to the Caribbean. An extremely religious man he was devoted to the Virgin Mary, and travelling north after making a landfall on Dominica he named a number of islands after her shrines. After departing from Guadeloupe, which he called Santa Maria de Guadeloupe, Columbus sailed up the leeside of Montserrat and named the island Santa Maria de Monserrate after a monastery near Barcelona. Montserrat is one of the few remaining British dependencies in the Caribbean and the inhabitants have a delightful Irish accent that is the legacy of Oliver Cromwell who, after destroying much of southern Ireland in the seventeenth century, exported some of his captives to Montserrat. Columbus did not drop anchor behind the island as presumably he could not find a good anchorage - the same is true today.

Montserrat's southern tip lies about 30 miles south west of English Harbour and about the same distance north west of Guadeloupe. Montserrat would make an ideal stop-over for a voyage between Antigua and Guadeloupe but, unfortunately, the three possible anchorages on the west coast of the island are very deep and, as the Atlantic swell penetrates behind the island, they are usually very uncomfortable. A further inconvenience is that yachts wishing to anchor have first to enter Montserrat at the capital, Plymouth, in the south of the island.

In the north of Montserrat it is possible to drop anchor in either Little Bay or Carr's Bay about a mile south of Northwest Bluff. This anchorage can be very unpleasant with big swells, especially when the wind is strong and from the north east. The next anchorage is in the middle of the island, just south of Old Road Bluff in Old Road Bay.

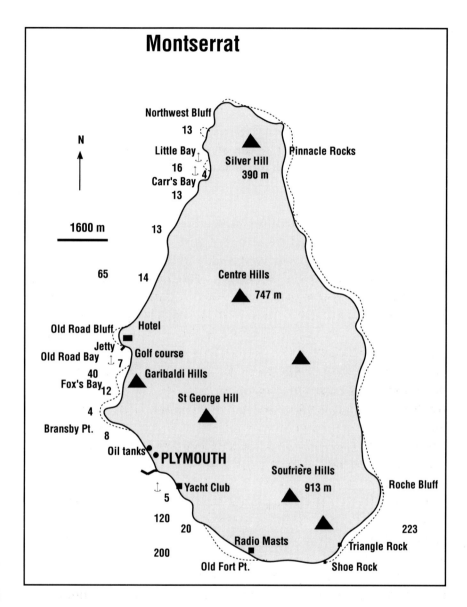

Yachts usually anchor in the north of Old Road Bay opposite the golf course and not far from the jetty.

Plymouth

The third and usually the most popular anchorage is just south of the town of Plymouth, opposite the yacht club and about a quarter of a mile south of Plymouth's landing dock for cargo ships. You are not allowed to anchor opposite the conspicuous Texaco oil tanks that are situated north of the main cargo ship dock.

Montserrat has a population of around 14 000 and Plymouth was once the home of the powerful Radio Antilles or 'Big RA' transmitter that broadcast two excellent daily marine weather forecasts. Unfortunately Big RA's radio masts were totally destroyed by Hurricane Hugo in 1989, and although a year later the radio station was back in action it was broadcasting at a much reduced power.

Customs and Immigration

Wherever you anchor in Montserrat you first have to enter the island at Plymouth. Customs are situated just off the main dock in Plymouth. They are closed Wednesday and Saturday afternoons, otherwise they are open from 0800 to 1200, and then from 1300 to 1600. Immigration is situated in the police station which is not far away.

Charts

British Admiralty: 254 General with detail of Plymouth
USA: 25601 General St Kitts to Montserrat
Imray Iolaire: A25 General with detail of Plymouth

Radio Station, Frequency and Times of Weather Bulletin

Radio Antilles: 930 kHz (0800,1830) Zone 3

GUADELOUPE

Guadeloupe was discovered by Columbus in 1493. Before he set out on his second voyage he had made a pilgrimage to the monastery in Guadalupe in Estremadura, Spain. He spent a long time praying in front of the Virgin of Guadalupe and the monks asked him to name an island after their monastery. As he approached Guadeloupe for the first time Columbus marvelled at the high Grand Carbet waterfall that seemed to come out of the clouds from high above the mountains, and he dropped anchor in Grand Anse at the foot of the 524 metres high Soufrière volcano in the south of the island. He fulfilled his promise to the monks and named the island - Santa Maria de Guadalupe.

The Caribs were firmly in control of the island when Columbus arrived and they called it Karukera or 'pretty waters island'. Guadeloupe was first colonised by France in 1635 and the settlers built their village on the western, leeward side of Guadeloupe not far from Grande Anse. Guadeloupe is split into two islands by a brackish river, the Rivière Salée, the western island is known as Basse Terre, the eastern island Grande Terre. The early French settlement on Basse Terre Island was known as Basse Terre, which today has become Guadeloupe's regional capital but not its largest town.

Guadeloupe fell to the English in 1759 who founded what is now the largest and most important urban area, Pointe à Pitre. The Treaty of Paris returned Guadeloupe to France in 1763, but the island was retaken by the English in 1794 only to be recaptured in the same year by Victor Hugues, a commissaire of the newly created French Republic. The slaves were freed and a 'reign of terror' followed as aristocrats and planters were guillotined by the revolutionaries.

Napoléon Bonaparte re-established slavery in 1802 (it was finally abolished in 1848) and some exiled colonial planters returned, but as a direct result of the French Revolution the island's aristocracy never recovered its former power. France lost the island after Napoleon's defeat but later regained it and, since 1816, Guadeloupe has remained French. In 1946 Guadeloupe became a French 'departement d'outre-mer' and like any other French departement, it is governed from Paris. Today, of Guadeloupe's 350 000 inhabitants, there are perhaps only 3 000 whites who can trace their ancestry back to the pre-revolution period, and a significant proportion of these whites, or 'Blanc-pays', is made up of Martiniquian whites or 'Bekes'. Unlike Guadeloupe, Martinique's aristocracy was not decimated by a reign of terror and in Martinique the Bekes still have a considerable amount of wealth and influence.

Guadeloupe is shaped like a butterfly. Basse Terre Island, the west wing of the Guadeloupe butterfly, is high, covered with tropical forests and dominated by the volcano Soufrière. Grande Terre Island, the east wing of the butterfly, is flatter, more cultivated and more populated. Pointe à Pitre has a population of 125 000. The French overseas department of Guadeloupe also includes the island dependencies of Marie Galante, Iles des Saintes, St Barthélemy and the north part of St Martin.

It is possible to sail south from Antigua to Guadeloupe to an anchorage off the small fishing village of Port Louis on the western, leeward side of the windward island Grande Terre, but this anchorage is open and subject to uncomfortable Atlantic swells. An alternative southern voyage from Antigua to Guadeloupe is through the reefs of Grand Cul de Sac Marin by the Passe à Colas to the Rivière Salée, eventually to reach the marina and anchorages around Pointe à Pitre. Most yachts use the Passe à Colas through the Grand Cul de Sac Marin to travel to Antigua from Guadeloupe, approaching the passage from the south via the Rivière Salée and Pointe à Pitre. However the north to south voyage is possible if you arrive off the middle of the Grand Cul de Sac Marin in good daylight (but I would not recommend this as you need to concentrate on eyeball reef navigation after what will probably have been a hard, long sail).

Enter the Passe à Colas from the north by first identifying the distinctive but low-lying Ilet à Fajou. The entrance to the Passe à Colas is about a mile north east of the island through two buoys, C1 and C2. Leave the red C1 buoy to starboard and the green C2 buoy to port and travel through the channel observing the usual 'red right returning rule'.

The most frequented cruising route of any Caribbean island is its leeward coast, and in Guadeloupe's case this is the west coast of the leeward island Basse Terre. There is a classical anchorage situated on the north west corner of Basse Terre at Deshaies (or Deshayes) Bay and this is the best and most visited of all Guadeloupe's many beautiful anchorages.

Anse Deshaies

The pretty, well-protected anchorage in Anse Deshaies is tucked away behind the steep-sided 208 metres high Gros Morne hill on the north of the bay. Most yachts rest up in Deshaies Bay either before or after tackling the crossing to Antigua or Montserrat.

Approach
When coming *from a northerly direction* the Ilet de Kahouanne and the smaller island to the north of it, the Tete à l'Anglais, stand out from the shore. Yachts can pass between these two islands and the mainland, but the whole area is full of fishing floats and there is an inshore shoal, La Perle, about a mile south of the Ilet de Kahouanne. Anse Deshaies is on the south side of Gros Morne. *From a northerly or southerly direction* the entrance to Anse Deshaies is easy by day and possible by night providing you are sure of your position and take care to avoid unlit yachts at anchor and the numerous hard-to-see fishing floats. In the village of Deshaies there is a conspicuous church.

Anchorage
This may be anywhere in the bay in depths of about 6 metres. Watch your depth sounder as the bottom comes up sharply. In season the anchorage can be crowded.

Ashore
There is a dinghy dock, and in the town there is a public laundry (bring your own plug), a selection of supermarkets, a post office, a bakery, a few restaurants and a municipal sports centre. Public buses run to Pointe à Pitre and Basse Terre but it is a long ride on a hard seat. Gas bottles can be exchanged at the petrol station.

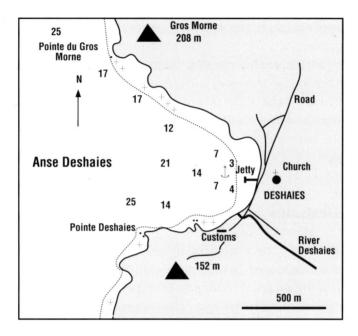

Customs and Immigration

A small customs office is situated on the south side of the village over the river and up the hill. The hours of opening are irregular.

The leeward coast of Basse Terre is steep-to and very deep. Yachts can approach within a quarter of a mile of the shore, which makes for an interesting voyage even when motor sailing in the frequent light and fluky winds that are typical of the leeward side of most Caribbean islands. Despite the very deep water close to the shore there are a number of good anchorages.

Pigeon or Goyave Islands

About 10 miles south of Anse Deshaies is Pigeon Island (actually two islands, one large and one small) which lies a short distance from the shore but can be passed on either side. If you are a keen scuba diver or an enthusiastic snorkeller there is an excellent anchorage in the bay opposite Pigeon Island since the island and the surrounding area are part of the famous Cousteau Underwater Reserve.

Approach

By day the approach is without difficulty *from either a northerly* (but mind the 2 metres shoal off Point Malendure) *or southerly direction,* but do not attempt this anchorage at night as Pigeon Island is unlit. Although underwater spearfishing is forbidden in the Cousteau Reserve - which includes Pigeon Island and a two square mile surrounding area - this does not prevent the local fishermen from setting fish traps with dozens of propellor-grabbing tiny white floats, so be on your guard.

Anchorage
Head up into the bay whose northern headland is Point Malendure and whose southern headland is Mount Criquet Point. Tuck yourself into the northern part of the bay and drop the anchor in about 4 metres of water opposite the jetty. The bottom is sand with the occasional rock. In the winter months when the wind is usually from a northerly direction the anchorage can be unpleasant because of the swell, and it is sometimes crowded.

Ashore
Much is aimed at divers visiting the Cousteau Underwater Reserve. There are glass bottomed boats, dive shops and restaurants.

Anse à la Barque

This anchorage is about 5 miles south of Pigeon Island and was at one time a busy banana port. It is a fine little deep-water bay that was once used as a hurricane hole by local craft from nearby Basse Terre. Although pretty and safe it only holds some half dozen yachts.

Approach
Easy from any direction. A lit, yellow concrete pylon marks the northern headland of the bay (Q (9) 15s 9M) but like many lights in the Caribbean it does not always work. The jetty at the head of the bay is in front of a white concrete sectored light (Fl (2) WRG 6s 8.5M) with 'Anse à la Barque' painted on the white in large green letters. This light's safe sector is white and the red sector shines over the unsafe rocky southern part of the bay.

Anchorage
Head towards the jetty and let go the anchor where you can. The anchorage is spoilt only by the sound of traffic on the nearby road.

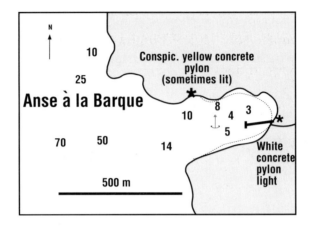

Ashore
Nothing in the way of facilities.

Basse Terre Roadstead

Basse Terre has a population of around 38 000 and is the largest town on Basse Terre Island. It is situated some six miles south of the Anse à la Barque anchorage and is a pleasant, quiet town not often visited by tourists. There is a small airport at nearby Baillif and a large commercial dock.

Approach
This poses no problem from any direction but watch out for the large mooring buoys some 300 metres off the L-shaped commercial dock.

Anchorage
Anchor either north or south of the dock in about 7 metres of water; the bottom comes up quite quickly. There is a sectored light on the dock (Fl WG 4s 9M) with white as the safe sector.

Ashore
All the amenities of a large town but for yacht chandleries you have to visit Pointe à Pitre which is a long bus ride away. In Guadeloupe there are shared 'taxis collectifs' that are much cheaper than the normal taxis. Collective taxis run on fixed routes and can be flagged down, but in Guadeloupe (unlike Martinique) they are less frequent than the buses.

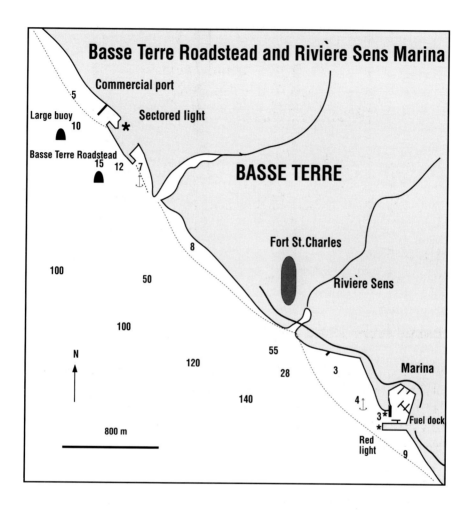

Basse Terre Roadstead and Rivière Sens Marina

Customs and Immigration

Basse Terre is a port of entry for Guadeloupe and the customs office is just off the large dock, alongside the tourist bureau. The bureau is not far from the Mairie.

Marina de Rivière Sens

The yacht anchorage off Basse Terre is an open roadstead and it is better to travel about a mile south past Fort St Charles (Richepanse) to the Marina de Rivière Sens. In 1979 Hurricane David almost destroyed the marina, but it was recently rebuilt and when Hurricane Hugo tore through Guadeloupe in 1989 fortunately there was little damage done. The berths in the marina are usually filled with local yachts but there is a good anchorage off its entrance.

Pointe du Vieux light, on the southern tip of Basse Terre, to port. Iles des Saintes ahead.

Approach

This poses no difficulty from any direction. Coming *from a northerly direction* simply follow the coast along from the town of Basse Terre.

The marina is situated below a very conspicuous quarry. When approaching *from a southerly direction* head in towards the shore after passing Vieux Fort Point lighthouse and identify the marina by the masts that appear above the harbour walls. The starboard entrance is lit with a red light and the port entrance with a green - but do not attempt to enter at night as you will probably be unable to find a berth.

Anchorage

Anchor in about 4 metres of water off the entrance. You can take the dinghy into the marina and it is quite safe to leave it moored to a pontoon.

Alongside and Ashore

Occasionally berths are available. There is a fuel dock just inside the starboard entrance where you can obtain diesel, water and ice, and ashore there is a small chandlery, a restaurant and a machine and rigging shop. If you need provisions it's up the road to Basse Terre where there are plenty of shops and supermarkets.

Customs and Immigration
The customs office is above the Port Captain's office opposite the main pontoon.

The wind usually increases and funnels round the final headlands of all the Caribbean islands, and the southern tip of Basse Terre is no exception. Once when we were travelling north and had just passed Vieux Fort Point lighthouse, the wind suddenly veered from north east to south and increased from a force three to a steady force seven. For over two hours we hissed along at hull speed on a completely flat sea - an incredible sail while it lasted.

Pointe à Pitre Harbour

The harbour at Pointe à Pitre is large, well protected and contains a number of safe yacht anchorages. The harbour is in a huge well-sheltered bay that lies to the north of Ilet à Cochons and between Grande and Basse Terre Islands. There is a commercial dock on Basse Terre Island, and on Grande Terre Island there is the largest and the best-equipped marina in the Lesser Antilles - the Marina du Bas du Fort. Often yachts cruising the classical north-south course route along the leeward side of the Caribbean island chain do not make the detour to Pointe à Pitre as it is some 20 miles to windward. But the sail need not be difficult - it all depends on the approach.

Approach
If approaching Pointe à Pitre *from the leeward side* of Basse Terre, it is possible to tack out into the channel that separates the Saintes islands and Guadeloupe (Canal des Saintes) and beat against the Atlantic swell and trade winds to Pointe à Pitre Harbour. But most cruising yachts prefer to head for the Iles des Saintes and rest at the delightful Bourg des Saintes anchorage before tackling the beat to Pointe à Pitre.

Yachts approaching Pointe à Pitre *from a southerly direction*, usually from Dominica, have a number of choices which, as is normally the

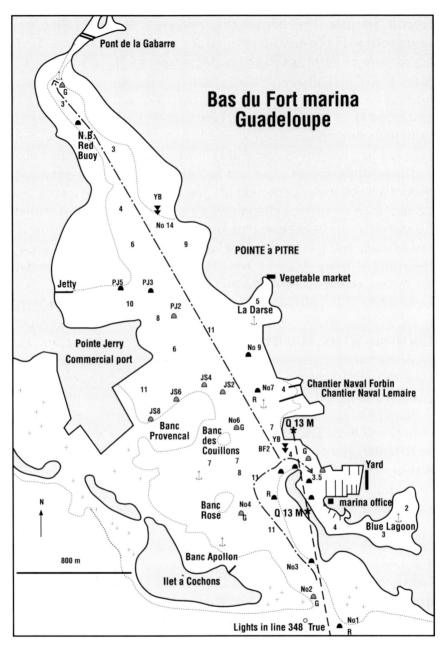

Bas du Fort marina Guadeloupe

Pont de la Gabarre

G
3

N.B. Red Buoy
3

YB
4
No 14

6   9

POINTE à PITRE

Jetty   PJ5   PJ3
10   PJ2   Vegetable market
8   5   La Darse
11

Pointe Jerry
Commercial port   6   No 9

JS4   JS2   No7   4   Chantier Naval Forbin
11   JS6   R   Chantier Naval Lemaire

JS8

Banc   Banc   No6   7   Q 13 M
Provencal   des   G   YB
Couillons   BF2   G
7   7   Yard
8   11   3.5

R   marina office   2

Banc   No4   Q 13 M
Rose   G   4   Blue Lagoon
11   3

800 m   Banc Apollon
No3
Ilet à Cochons

No2
G

Lights in line 348° True   No1
R

N

case, depend upon the strength and direction of the wind. The easiest voyage is to sail the 20 odd miles from the northern tip of Dominica to the anchorages in the Iles des Saintes and rest there before sailing on to Pointe à Pitre. In the summer months the trade winds are lighter and more southerly and yachts sometimes sail from Dominica to Marie Galante. From Marie Galante it is an easy reach to Pointe à

Pitre. If you have a powerful, weatherly yacht it is quite possible to sail directly to Pointe à Pitre from Dominica.

Transatlantic yachts arriving from the east have no problems with the wind, and the marina at Pointe à Pitre is occasionally used for the finish of important ocean races. Some French cruising yachts make a landfall on Marie Galante before sailing on to Guadeloupe.

The final approach in to Pointe à Pitre harbour is extremely well marked, but the lights and buoys have been designed for large merchant ships and they are not easy to sort out from the moving deck of a small yacht - especially if approaching at night against the lights of a town the size of Pointe à Pitre. Thus, for the first visit to the harbour, it is best to enter by day.

Approaching *from any southerly direction* identify and clear Point Capesterre, keeping a mile or so offshore if beating up from the Iles des Saintes. Continue up towards the Petit Cul de Sac and do not be tempted by the difficult anchorage off the town of Sainte Marie. There is a very conspicuous wreck on the Caye Dupont, which should be left well to port. Identify the collection of buoys that mark the deep water West Channel to Pointe à Pitre and the 3 metre Mouchoir Carre shoal. This shoal lies just to the east of the last red buoy of the West Channel.

The safest approach to Pointe à Pitre Harbour is to leave the large, lit (Iso 4s 9M) red and white 'PP' buoy to port. The white lighthouse on Gosier Island (Fl (2) R 10s 15M) with its red top stands out clearly from the shore. Head for the channel between the Ilet à Cochons and Grande Terre Island, entering it between the lit (Q R) No 1 red, starboard hand buoy and the lit No 2 green, port hand buoy (Fl G 6s). Pointe à Pitre's leading lights come into transit on 348° True, and both are white and quick flashing with a range of 13 miles (Q 13M). Leave the transit and pass No 3 red buoy to starboard. If making for the marina, leave two more red buoys to starboard and then turn into the entrance which is marked by a red and green buoy. There is a lit (Q (6)+L Fl 15s) yellow and black Cardinal South BF2 buoy just north of the entrance.

Marina and Anchorage

The 'Quai d'Accueil' for visiting yachts is just north of the fuelling dock. Tie up there and obtain a berth number from the marina office. There are mooring buoys (or 'corps morts') available at half the price of the pontoon berths and yachts wishing to anchor in the

Lagon Blue, which has a minimum depth of about 2 metres, have to obtain permission from the marina office. If the Quai d'Accueil is full go alongside the first, A6, pontoon.

Other anchorages

One is on the the north side of the Ilet à Cochons in depths of about 5 metres. Another is off the two large shipyards (Chantier Naval Forbin and Chantier Naval Lemarie) which are situated in the first bay north of the marina. These yards have two railways that can haul yachts displacing 20 tons and up to 12 metres long, as well as four floating dry docks, with the largest capable of lifting a vessel displacing 750 tons. It is possible to anchor in the next bay north, La Darse, but the water is dirty, there is no breeze and the busy inter-island ferries berth in this bay.

Alongside and Ashore

At Bas du Fort Marina water, ice, diesel and petrol can be obtained from the fuel dock. There are 660 berths with electricity (110/220V) and water and the cost is around 180 FF per 10 metres per night. Telephones, a telex and a poste restante (address: Yacht <>, Poste Restante, Port de Plaisance, Marina Bas du Fort, Guadeloupe, French West Indies) are all conveniently located near the marina office. In the north east corner of the marina there is an industrial zone which has a wide range of yacht-orientated businesses and a modern 27 ton travel-lift. In the marina complex are yacht charterers, laundries, bars, restaurants, boutiques and supermarkets as well as a chemist, two marine electronic shops and three excellent chandleries. The centre of Point à Pitre is about 45 minutes walk from the marina but it is also possible to take the dinghy to La Darse bay. Not far from this bay is the large, well stocked Electro Navic chandlery.

In La Darse bay the inshore fishermen sell their morning's catch from their brightly painted boats. Stretching away from the waterfront is a busy colourful vegetable market. In the attractive, well laid out centre of Pointe à Pitre there are museums, a fine park and a variety of sophisticated shops, French-style bars and some excellent restaurants.

Customs and Immigration

These are adjacent to the marina office.

Rivière Salée

About two miles north of the marina is the entrance to the salt river that divides Guadeloupe into two and which offers a good alternative route to Antigua from Dominica or the Iles des Saintes. There is, however, one problem in that the southern entrance to the river is crossed by a bridge, the Pont de la Gabarre, which opens only once a day, and that's at 0530! While it is possible to leave the Bas du Fort marina at dawn and motor up to the bridge in uncertain daylight to be in time for the 0530 opening, it is preferable to arrive the day before and anchor close to the bridge, taking care to avoid the remains of the old bridge. There is an anchorage on the other side of the bridge for yachts travelling south. When travelling up to the bridge from the marina, before Pointe à Pitre leave all red buoys to starboard. But once past La Darse anchorage, the IALA Buoyage System B changes direction, and vessels are now assumed to be *returning* to Pointe à Pitre, thus red buoys have to be left on the port bow.

The Rivière Salée is a passage through a mangrove swamp with channel depths that range from about 3 to 5 metres. Many yachts tied themselves to the mangroves during the passage of Hurricane Hugo in 1989 and many were damaged. At one time during the hurricane it was estimated that a seven knot current was flowing through the river, and much of the yacht damage was caused by yachts breaking adrift and crashing into one another. Keep to the centre of the river and, providing you draw less than 2.7 metres and your mast is less than 24.4 metres (there is an overhead electric cable just north of the bridge) you will find the passage well marked and easy. Do not forget to leave the red marks to port and green to starboard when travelling north. The last, red, northern river buoy is marked RS1 where it enters the Passe à Colas, which is the name of the passage through the numerous coral reefs of the Grand Cul de Sac Marin. As you emerge from the Rivière Salée when voyaging north, make sure you identify the next red, port hand buoy C9 that is situated slightly east of RS1. If you do not, there is a good chance you will run aground on the muddy shoal just north of RS1. There is a convenient anchorage just south of the green channel buoy C6 which lies south of the tiny Ilet Colas, situated east of Ilet à Fajou. The water is reasonably clear, so carefully choose your spot away from coral and weed before anchoring in about 7 metres of water.

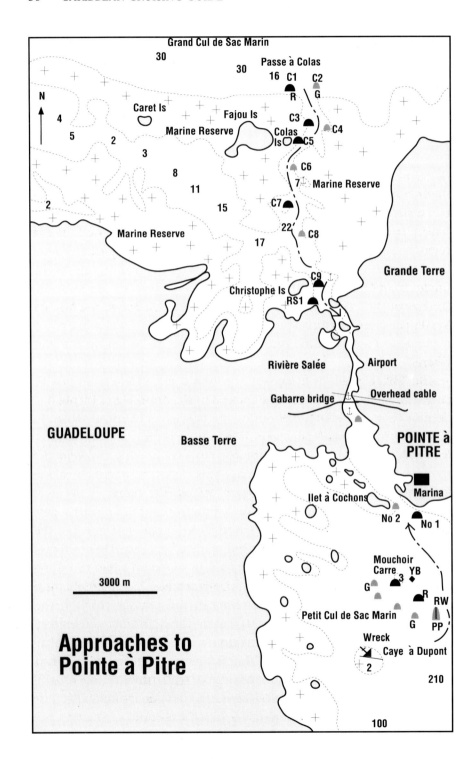

Grand Cul de Sac Marin

30

30

Passe à Colas

16 C1   C2
        R   G

N

4

5   2

Caret Is

Fajou Is

Marine Reserve

C3

Colas
Is   C5

C4

3

8

11

2

15

C6

7   Marine Reserve

C7

22   C8

Marine Reserve

17

Grande Terre

C9

Christophe Is

RS1

Rivière Salée

Airport

Gabarre bridge

Overhead cable

GUADELOUPE

Basse Terre

POINTE à
PITRE

Marina

Ilet à Cochons

No 2   No 1

3000 m

Mouchoir
Carre 3 YB

G

R

RW

Petit Cul de Sac Marin

G   PP

Wreck

**Approaches to
Pointe à Pitre**

Caye à Dupont

2

210

100

Yachts sometimes anchor behind the Ilet du Gosier with its distinctive lighthouse. The entrance is simple providing you keep well north of the Ilet before turning west into the shelter behind the reefs. Anchor in sandy clay in about 3 metres of water. There is a conspicuous church spire in the town of Gosier behind the lighthouse and up the steep hill.

Other anchorages exist off the south coast of Grande Terre (Petit Havre, Sainte Anne, St François) but they are off the classical route and usually involve a beat against the wind and an entrance through a reef. The entrance to the anchorage between the Isles de la Petite Terre is difficult and dangerous and should not be attempted.

Customs and Immigration
For any of these anchorages enter or leave Guadeloupe at the Marina Bas du Fort (see above).

Charts
French: 3423 General
British Admiralty: 885 General, 491 Details, 804 Approaches Pointe à Pitre
USA: 25563 General, 25566 Approaches Pointe à Pitre
Imray Iolaire: A28 General and Details

Radio Station, Frequency and Times of Weather Bulletin
RFO: 640 kHz (0620,1830,1900)
RCL: 1210 kHz

Airport
International airport at the town of Abymes north of Pointe à Pitre
Tel: 828080

MARIE GALANTE

Flush with the success of his first voyage Columbus set out in 1493 on his second attempt to sail to the East Indies.The monarchs of Spain had given him a 17-ship fleet and the new flagship was the *Santa Maria*, named after the ship Columbus lost on his first voyage - the sailors affectionately called her the *Mariagalante*. Land was sighted after 21 days at sea, but it was Dominica's steep windward coast where there are no harbours. Altering course to starboard the fleet saw a low flat island ahead, and working their way over to the leeside of the island the fleet finally dropped anchor. Columbus went ashore and called the island Mariagalante, in honour of his flagship.

Marie Galante lies south of St François on Grande Terre and some 15 miles east of the Iles des Saintes. Columbus saw these islands to leeward of Marie Galante, and as the feast of All Saints had just passed he named them Todos los Santos.

Before electricity arrived flat Marie Galante was known as the 'island of 100 windmills'. Today Marie Galante is a quiet island of some 20 000 inhabitants well off the tourist track and most famous for its sugar cane fields, the ox carts that take the cut cane to the distilleries and a delicious white rum - rhum agricole du Père Labat. A rum that, like all white rums, is distilled from the juice extracted from crushed sugar cane and bottled and drunk before it is aged. Rhum Père Labat is considered by many Frenchmen to be the best 'rhum agricole' in the Caribbean. On mainland Guadeloupe and Martinique some of the best quality white rums obtained from the juice of crushed cane are aged in wooden casks. After a number of years the white rum turns brown and becomes known as 'vieux rhum' - old rum - which can be as silky smooth and aromatic as the best French brandies. The ex-British colonies also produce dark rums but these excellent tasting rums, from, for example, Barbados and Jamaica, are brown not because they are cask aged but because they are made from molasses (caramelised sugar) obtained from the sugar cane.

The island of Marie Galante can be approached from Pointe à Pitre, but if the wind is blowing from the south east it can be a long beat. The main yacht anchorage is off the town of St Louis in the south of the island and in the summer months, when the trade winds are lighter and more southerly, this anchorage can often be reached in one tack from the north leeward coast of the island of Dominica.

Saint Louis anchorage

Approach
This presents no problem during the day. Yachts coming *from Guadeloupe or the north* will be able to identify rocky, Vieux Fort Island and, keeping clear of the rocks off Pointe du Cimetière, head down towards the new long ferry jetty in the middle of the bay. When *approaching from the south and west* there is a conspicuous jetty off Pointe de Folle Anse which has an enormous crane for loading and unloading cargo ships. There are oil tanks close to the new ferry jetty that runs out from the town of St Louis. At the town end of the jetty there is a prominent war memorial as well as a light (Fl G 4s 8M).

Anchorage
Most yachts anchor on the south side of the ferry jetty in depths of 2 to 5 metres, but it is possible to drop the anchor anywhere in this well sheltered bay as long as you keep clear of the pipes that run from the storage tanks to a red buoy just west of the jetty. Yachts occasionally go alongside the jetty but it is high and you will have difficulty setting fenders.

Pointe du Vieux Fort
Vieux Fort Is
8
Pointe du Cimetière
N
13
8 2
SAINT LOUIS
8 R *Fl G 4s 8M
Fuel storage tanks
Pointe de Folle Anse
6
Loading dock, fuel reservoirs and crane
10
1500 m
4
28 8 St Louis Anchorage Marie Galante
64

Ashore

The small village has a post office with telephones, a couple of restaurants where you have to pre-order, bars and a couple of small supermarkets. Collective taxis stop outside the post office and run up to the island's regional capital, Grand Bourg, where there is a regular ferry service to Pointe à Pitre and the Iles des Saintes. A small yacht basin has recently been built on the east side of the ferry dock at Grand Bourg. The entrance is through a buoyed passage through the reef (remember red buoys kept to starboard when entering) but the Atlantic swell manages to creep inside the new harbour walls and the anchorage is not recommended.

Customs and Immigration

There is a police station or gendarmerie at St Louis and another at Grand Bourg. Neither become very excited about entering and clearing yachts, but it is worthwhile visiting either one of them with a crew list and the ship's papers just to say that you have been. There is an anchorage in the next bay north of Saint Louis at Anse Carnot, but swell can make it uncomfortable and it is not as good as the anchorage in Saint Louis Bay.

Charts

British Admiralty: 491 Details
USA: 25564 General Iles des Saintes, 25565 Marie Galante
Imray Iolaire: A281 General and Details Iles des Saintes and Marie Galante

ILES DES SAINTES

From Marie Galante it is always a wonderful downwind sail to the Iles des Saintes. This is a group of six, small, delightful islands of which only two are inhabited, Terre d'en Haut and Terre d'en Bas. Discovered by Columbus in 1493 they became famous in British naval history for the Battle of the Saints. In 1782 the Comte de Grasse sailed from Martinique with 34 ships of the line and 5 500 soldiers in an attempt to link his French forces with the Spanish and overrun the British bases on Jamaica. However, the French fleet was surprised by Sir George Rodney off the Iles des Saintes, and Rodney, with 35 British ships of the line, won such a convincing victory that French power in the West Indies was broken for a long time.

Anse du Bourg

Approach
By day the approach *from the north or south* is without undue difficulty. The classical anchorage is off the town of Bourg des Saintes situated on the largest eastern island, Terre d'en Haut.

If you are *sailing from Dominica* you should approach the anchorage through the easiest of the southern passages - the south west passage or Passe du Sud Ouest. Steer a course that puts you just east of the west end of Terre d'en Bas: this island will be quite close before the much smaller islands of La Coche and Les Augustins become distinct, and the passage between Les Augustins and Terre d'en Bas opens up. Pass the conspicuous Pain de Sucre hill to starboard and head towards the town avoiding the 1.3 metre shoal

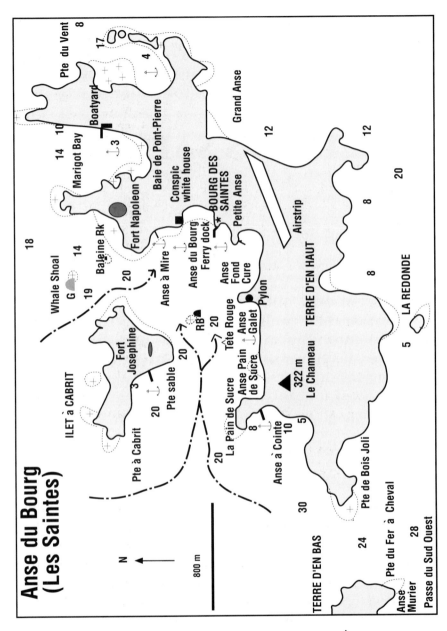

Anse du Bourg (Les Saintes)

Pte du Vent · 8 · 17 · 4 · Boatyard · 10 · 14 · Marigot Bay · 3 · Baie de Pont-Pierre · Conspic white house · Grand Anse · 12 · 12 · 20 · Fort Napoleon · BOURG DES SAINTES · Petite Anse · Airstrip · 8 · Baleine Rk · Anse du Bourg Ferry dock · 18 · Whale Shoal · G · 14 · 19 · 20 · Anse à Mire · Anse Fond Cure · Pylon · TERRE D'EN HAUT · 8 · LA REDONDE · Fort Josephine · RB · Tête Rouge · 20 · Anse Galet · 5 · ILET à CABRIT · 20 · Pte sable · 20 · Anse Pain de Sucre · 322 m · Le Chameau · Pte à Cabrit · 20 · La Pain de Sucre · 8 · Pte de Bois Joli · 20 · Anse à Cointe · 10 · 5 · N · 800 m · 30 · TERRE D'EN BAS · 24 · Pte du Fer à Cheval · 28 · Anse Murier · Passe du Sud Ouest

that lies about half way between the Ilet à Cabit and Tête Rouge Point on Terre d'en Haut Island. The shoal is marked with an unlit, red and black buoy and there is deep water on either side of the shoal.

Yachts approaching the Saintes *from the leeward side of Basse Terre* should enter Anse du Bourg by day via the easy, safe passage that lies between the small island of La Pate and the Ilet à Cabrit.

When approaching the anchorage *from the east* there is a small passage between Ilet à Cabrit and Whale Shoal (Baleine du Large) which is marked by a green buoy. Do not, as I once did when the French were in the middle of changing over from the European to the American system of buoyage, put the green Whale Shoal buoy on the starboard bow when approaching the anchorage. (I missed the rocky shoal by a fraction, travelling too fast under full sail - it was the closest I have ever come to losing a boat). The buoy is now green and must be left to port when entering the Anse du Bourg - the American system of 'red right returning' - and it is lit (Fl G (2) 6s). Watch for the dangerous, unlit, Whale Rock (La Baleine) which rises about 1 metre out of the water and lies south east of Whale Shoal. When coming from the east the safest route is to sail past the Ilet à Cabrit and enter the anchorage from the north west, between Ilet à Cabrit and La Pate.

The anchorage off the town of Bourg des Saintes on Terre d'en Haut Island has a sectored light at the head of the ferry jetty (Fl WRG 4s 29ft 10 7M). The white safe sector shines over the Whale Passage but I would not advise using this passage at night.

Anchorage
Most yachts anchor north of the town's ferry dock and south of the 'doctor's house', which is white and shaped like the bow of a ship. Keep the passage clear to the ferry dock and anchor in a depth of about 7 metres. Use a depth sounder as the bottom comes up fairly sharply from around 20 metres - and be prepared to have trouble digging in the anchor.

There is another anchorage below Fort Napoleon in Anse à Mire about a quarter of a mile north of the ferry dock. Large passenger ships sometimes anchor near the Ilet à Cabrit, and the bay becomes very busy as the ships' lifeboats discharge and load passengers at the ferry dock. It is best to leave your dinghy on the jetty, opposite the small outdoor market in Bourg and just south of the ferry dock. There is a small jetty in the north corner of Anse à Mire if you decide to anchor below Fort Napoleon.

Yachts can also drop anchor south of Bourg in Petite Anse, and in the next bay south in Anse Fond Cure. West of Tête Rouge Point there is an anchorage in Anse Galet and behind Sugar Loaf hill, or Pain de Sucre, there is a calm but often crowded spot in Anse à Cointe. There is also a quiet anchorage off the southern coast of Ilet à Cabrit, just west of Fort Louis or Fort Josephine as it is locally known.

Alongside and Ashore

The islands are very beautiful and the town of Bourg des Saintes is picturesque and quiet - until the ferries and passenger ships arrive. There are no facilities for taking on either diesel or water at the town jetty. There are numerous restaurants in and near the town, tiny supermarkets, a post office, a bakery, a bank that opens infrequently, car and scooter hire shops and telephones. There is a regular ferry service between Bourg des Saintes and Pointe à Pitre. Fort Josephine on Ilet à Cabrit is derelict but worth visiting, as is the well-restored Fort Napoleon on Terre d'en Haut. If you have the energy, a difficult scramble up the 606 metres high Pain de Sucre gives magnificent views, as does the climb up to the top of the old Napoleonic watch tower at Le Chameau, south east of the Pain de Sucre. There is a beautiful windward beach on Terre d'en Haut below Windy Point (Pointe du Vent) and not far from Bourg des Saintes in the Baie de Pont-Pierre. This bay is also a yacht anchorage with a rather hair-raising entrance. The locals use it as a hurricane hole, tucking themselves into the head of the bay in 4 metres of water.

Terre d'en Haut has a well equipped boatyard on the east shores of Marigot Bay. From the Bourg anchorage head out through the passage between Whale Shoal and the Ilet à Cabrit, motor sail along the coast, giving the L'Eau headland that lies below Fort Napoléon a good clearance, before turning to starboard to enter Marigot Bay. The trip is not easy as you will be against wind and sea. The Roche à Move yard is about halfway down on the east side of Marigot Bay; you can anchor off in depths of around 3 metres. In northerly winds the anchorage is unpleasant because of the swell. The yard can supply a sailmaker, a rigger, welders and it has an engine repair shop. The yard is in a beautiful spot but it is not cheap and you are not allowed to work on your own boat. There is a restaurant at the head of the bay.

Customs and Immigration

The same relaxed attitude prevails here as at Marie Galante. Take the ship's papers to the gendarmerie just opposite the ferry jetty.

Charts

British Admiralty: 491 Details
USA: 25564 General Iles des Saintes, 25565 Marie Galante
Imray Iolaire: A281 General and Details Iles des Saintes and Marie Galante.

DOMINICA

Beautiful, sad, much maligned, majestic Dominica. The island lies south of the Iles des Saintes and north of Martinique and is one of the largest, most mountainous, green, lush and beautiful of all the islands in this guide. It is also one of the poorest, being continuously devastated by hurricanes, and, with almost no white sand beaches, the island earns little from tourism. Because it is so high it rains continuously on Dominica - throughout the dry and wet Caribbean seasons. The roads are washed away. The tourists fail to come; but they are missing much. Dominica's rich tropical forests are lit with frequent rainbows, criss-crossed by bubbling streams and full of brightly coloured flowers, butterflies and birds.

Dominica was Columbus' second landfall in the Caribbean. One November Sunday in 1493 after 21 days at sea his ships sighted land, and Columbus named his landfall island Dominica. But he did not stop, and instead sailed north to anchor behind Marie Galante. Had he landed he would have been greeted by hostile Caribs. Because of the thick rain forests and high mountains, colonising Europeans had great trouble in subduing these fiercely independent Indians, and Dominica is one of the few Caribbean islands where the Caribs were not deported or totally exterminated. Today there is a Carib reserve on the windward side of the island where some 500 Caribs make a meagre living selling souvenirs to the few tourists. Dominica, placed between the French islands of Guadeloupe and Martinique, became an important strategic prize in the long power struggle between France and Britain. It changed hands several times and finally became a British colony in 1783, remaining so until Dominica became a fully independent republic in 1978.

Portsmouth, Prince Rupert Bay, Dominica

Today there are some 80 000 inhabitants living on the island, mostly descendants of African slaves, and 20 000 live in the island's capital, Roseau. There are excellent anchorages in the north of the island in well-sheltered Prince Rupert Bay. In the south there are two fair anchorages, one of which makes a reasonable overnight stop.

Prince Rupert Bay

There are two popular anchorages in this beautiful bay which is over two miles wide - one in the north of the bay, between East Cabrit Hill and the town of Portsmouth, and the other in the south opposite the Coconut Beach Hotel. Under settled conditions yachts can anchor close to the shore at almost any point within the bay, and quite a number choose to moor off the town of Portsmouth. Your arrival will probably be greeted by a number of vociferous youngsters paddling broken windsurfers with pieces of wood or by their elder brothers in outboard-driven boats offering you fresh fruit or trips up the Indian River. These 'boat boys' have a bad reputation with cruising sailors, and they can be over-persistent and a nuisance. But compared with the average yachtsman they are very poor and they are only out to obtain work. In my experience if you are always polite and honest with them you will rarely have trouble. Do not try to set boat against boat and always keep your part of any bargain you strike. The boat boys can be very helpful, especially if you are on passage and do not want to spend time ashore; they will obtain very quickly reasonably-priced fresh fruit and bread. I have sometimes paid half the negotiated price before receiving the goods and have never been let down. For around $20 EC a head the boat boys will take you up the Indian River which is well worth a visit.

Approach

From the north the sail between Dominica and the Iles des Saintes is straightforward; do not forget to allow for the one to two knot west-going current. Steer for West Cabrit, which rises steeply from Prince Rupert Bluff, and although some 190 metres high stands out as a low hill against the background of Dominica's high mountains. The northern anchorage in Prince Rupert Bay lies behind the West and East Cabrit hills. Round the headland and anchor about half way between Prince Rupert Bluff and the town of Portsmouth which has a conspicuous church. The eye of Hurricane David went through the south of the island and in 1989 the eye of Hurricane Hugo went very close to the north of the island. During Hugo, waves broke right across the bay and carried a cargo ship ashore just in front of the town of Portsmouth.

When approaching *from the south*, some 20 miles after passing the island's capital Roseau and a probable motor sail up the windless leeward side of the island, you round Rollo Head and enter Prince Rupert Bay. A wind often blows out of the bay and it has the annoying habit of always seeming to be on the nose.

Anchorage

The anchorages in the north and south parts of the bay are in good holding, muddy sand in about 6 metres of water. In the north yachts generally drop anchor in the north east of the bay (see sketch chart), off the Purple Turtle Beach bar - which has a very loud jump-up on a Friday night. You can leave your dinghy here and walk into Portsmouth. Dinghys can also be left at Sunshine Village dock about a quarter of a mile east of Fort Shirley where a project is underway to build a small marina.

If you are concerned about theft leave your dinghy by the ruins of the main jetty near the police station. There have been thefts from unattended yachts moored in Prince Rupert Bay.

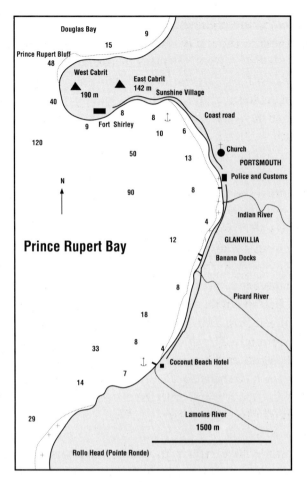

The anchorage in the south of the Prince Rupert Bay is in about 5 metres of water off the Coconut Beach Hotel whose name is clearly written in black lettering on a low wall that runs in front of the hotel.

Ashore

Portsmouth is a poor town, but there is a vegetable market on Saturday where fruit is very cheap - especially the grapefruit, limes and bananas. In town there is a bank, a bakery, and a few small shops selling mostly tinned food. It is possible to organise a trip to the Carib reservation and other trips into the interior. Do not forget about the trip up the Indian River, and Fort Shirley which is being restored and is situated below the Cabrits is also worth a visit.

The Coconut Beach Hotel anchorage offers a beach, a happy hour at the beach bar and restaurant, a shower at the hotel and diving enthusiasts can arrange scuba trips.

Customs and Immigration

Present yourself at the police station in Portsmouth near the ruined jetty. They are open during the week from 0800 to 1200 and from 1300 to 1600. Yachts entering or clearing outside these hours have to pay an overtime fee.

Dominica's leeward coast is steep-to and a quarter of a mile offshore clears all dangers. There is usually little wind though occasional squalls come roaring down from the mountain tops. If weather conditions are settled it is possible to anchor for an overnight stop at a number of different locations between Rupert Bay and the anchorages in the south of Dominica. For example:

  • below Barber's Block, just south of Rollo Head
  • off the Grand Savanna
  • off the River Layou that runs though the town of Hillsborough (one anchorage about 1½ miles north of the mouth of the river, and one just north of the river off the village of Layou)
  • on the north side of the mouth of the River Boery, which is easily identified from the sea by the two large cement silos that are situated on the south side of the river mouth.

Roseau and the Anchorage Hotel

The Anchorage Hotel is situated about a mile and a quarter south east of the River Roseau that runs through the capital. The hotel is easily identified by the black lettering on a white wall, and the anchorage is a convenient overnight stop before tackling the often rough passage between Dominica and Martinique. Yachts approaching the anchorage *from a southerly direction* should head for Roseau after passing Cachacrou or Scott's Head, being careful to avoid the rocky shoals that lie some 400 metres off Scott's Head.

Approach

By day with ease *from either the north or the south*. The bottom comes up sharply but there is a reasonably wide shelf on which to anchor in sticky, black sand in a depth of about 6 metres. Take a stern line ashore to the mooring post off the hotel a local boatman will be happy to run out the line for a fee of $5 EC. It is possible to anchor just north of the hotel without a stern line but the weather has, of course, to be settled.

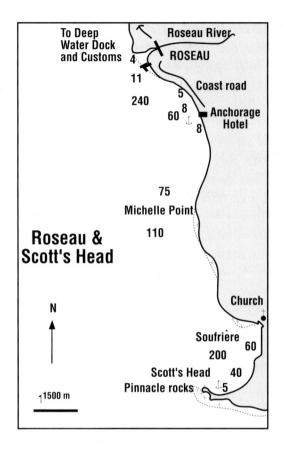

To Deep Water Dock and Customs
Roseau River
ROSEAU
4
11
Coast road
5
240
8
60
Anchorage Hotel
8

75
Michelle Point
110

**Roseau &
Scott's Head**

N

1500 m

Church

Soufrière
200
60

Scott's Head   40
Pinnacle rocks   5

Ashore

At the hotel there are showers, laundry facilities, telephones, a fresh water swimming pool and a restaurant where you can dine and look down on to your boat. From the hotel you can plan night time scuba dives; tours to the Trafalgar Falls, Middleham Waterfall, Emerald Pool and the Boiling Lake; a visit to the Carib Reservation in the north of the island and an outing to nearby Roseau. In Roseau there are a number of supermarkets, banks, chemists, restaurants, a post office, souvenir shops and a tourist office. The Botanical Gardens in the south part of town are of interest, as is Morne Trois Pitons Park which has a number of interesting walks.

Customs and Immigration

Yachts have to enter Dominica at the customs and immigration offices situated on the main dock of the deep water harbour in Woodbridge Bay, which is about a mile north of the mouth of the River Roseau (or Queen's River). Yachts can anchor off the deep water harbour, but make sure that you leave access to the Deep Water Docks and the more northern Banana Docks. Before dropping the anchor call the Harbour Master on VHF ch 16 to obtain permission to anchor. Yachts can anchor north and south of the mouth of Roseau River but it is always better to head down to the Anchorage Hotel.

Scott's Head

A possible anchorage is behind Scott's Head in the extreme south of Dominica. Anchor just off the strip of land that connects the 71.3 metres high hill to the mainland in Soufrière Bay. The shelf is narrow and the holding poor so be careful. When approaching this anchorage *from the north* give the shoal off the village of Soufrière a wide berth, and when coming in *from the south* to Soufrière Bay keep some 400 metres off the shoal that lies west north west of Scott's Head.

The passage between Dominica and Martinique is about 26 miles and although usually a reach, the seas can be rough. The wind speeds up as it swirls round the southern half of Dominica and can be 10 to 20 knots stronger for the first few miles of the voyage than it is in the middle of the passage. The current is west going and sometimes runs at two knots.

Charts
French: 3775 General
British Admiralty: 696 General, 728 Details
USA: 26562 General, 25562 Details
Imray Iolaire: A29 General

Radio Station, Frequency and Times of Weather Bulletin
Radio Dominica: 595 kHz

Airport
Carefield Airport at Roseau, also a small airstrip at Nelville Hall in the north of the island.

MARTINIQUE

'It is the best, the most fertile, the sweetest, the most charming country in the world. It is the most beautiful thing I have ever seen and I could tire my eyes contemplating such greenery', wrote Columbus after he had made a landfall on Martinique in 1502 during his fourth voyage, and that was after 10 years of discoveries in the West Indies. When Columbus arrived the island was inhabited by the Caribs, and Martinique probably owes its name to the Carib word 'Madinina', the island of flowers.

The first inhabitants in Martinique were Amerindians who arrived around 180 AD. They were replaced around 300 AD by the Arawaks, and the Caribs arrived around 850 AD. In 1635 a French buccaneer, Belain d'Esnambuc, arrived from the French settlement in Saint Christopher (St Kitts) and took possession of Martinique in the name of the French Company of Saint Christopher. The French settlers built Fort Saint Pierre in the north of the island at the foot of Mount Pelée and in 1675 the island became an official French colony. At first friendly relationships were developed with the Caribs who lived on the windward side of the island, but later the Caribs were either exterminated or exported and the French colonists imported African slaves to work the tobacco and sugar cane plantations. The adventuresome Dominican friar Père Labat arrived in Martinique in 1693, stayed until 1705, and wrote about sugar cane production and the island's fort in his wonderful book *Voyages aux Iles d'Amérique*.

In 1762 England captured the island but swapped it for Canada in the following year at the Treaty of Paris. In 1794 Martinique was recaptured by the English but Napoleon Bonaparte retook the island in 1802, no doubt spurred on by the Empress Josephine who was born on the island at Trois Ilets in 1763 (just avoiding being born a British citizen!). Napoléon lost the island in 1809 but in 1814 it was handed back to the French by the Second Treaty of Paris, and since then Martinique has remained French. In 1946 during the international post-war shedding of colonies Martinique became a French departement d'outre-mer - an overseas department - and is considered to be part of France. It is governed from Paris, although there is some degree of autonomy, and French wealth has been poured into the island with the result that Martinique has become one of the most developed of all the Windward Islands with the highest standard of living.

Like most of the Caribbean islands in this guide, tourism has largely replaced the tobacco and the sugar cane industries. The east coast, or windward side of the island, has few beaches and the sand is an uninviting black. As a result there are few tourist attractions and, as is common with most other Caribbean islands, there are no classical anchorages. The west coast, leeward side, has tourism, white sand and a good number of anchorages.

The total population of Martinique, most of whom are black or mulatto people, is about 320 000. Almost a third of the total number of the inhabitants live in the capital, Fort de France, which is also the principal town and port. Throughout the island the language is either French or Créole, a complex dialect of French, tribal African, Spanish and English. Créole is a written language and reflects the Caribbean history of slavery, colonial invasion and counter invasion; to the French-speaking European, Créole is largely incomprehensible. Fort de France is a hot, bustling town and a large deep-water container port. It is often on the itinerary of the increasing numbers of cruise ships that ply the Caribbean islands. Because of the port's links with Europe, Fort de France is one of the best provisioned towns in the Windward Islands and offers first class facilities for the cruising yacht. Yachts entering Martinique usually do so at Fort de France, but they also have the choice of Marin, Trinite'or Saint Pierre.

Fort de France became Martinique's principal town after the settlement that grew up around Fort St Pierre was completely destroyed in 1902 when, almost without warning, volcanic Mount Pelée erupted. Out of 14 ships at anchor, 13 were sunk. The town was flattened and its 30 000, mostly white, inhabitants were asphyxiated by poisonous gases - the only person to survive was a black prisoner held in a thick-walled cell.

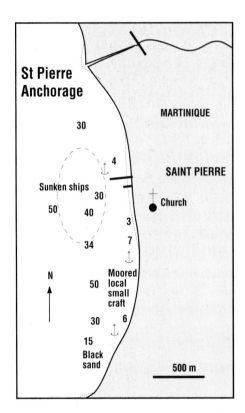

St Pierre
Anchorage

MARTINIQUE

30

4

SAINT PIERRE

Sunken ships
30
50   40

+ Church

3
7
34

N

Moored
50   local
small
craft

30   6

15
Black
sand

500 m

Saint Pierre

Saint Pierre is a safe overnight resting place before or after tackling the often rough, passage between Martinique and Dominica.

Approach

By day no difficulty from any direction. Wrecks of ships sunk by the eruption of Mount Pelée are covered by at least 10 metres of water. Saint Pierre has a distinctive church; head for the dock off the town centre, north of the church. A brightly illuminated statue is situated on the hill south of the town.

Anchorage

This is on a narrow sandy shelf in a depth of about 8 metres just off the dock. There is an alternative and equally good anchorage south of the dock in depths of 5 to 8 metres and just north of the fishing boats' moorings. The bottom is hard black sand and is sometimes difficult to penetrate with a CQR anchor. A swell can enter the bay and cause anchored yachts to roll unpleasantly

Ashore

Dinghies can be safely left at the jetty, and most provisions can be obtained from the town of about 6 000 inhabitants. There are restaurants and bars, and for the experienced scuba diver dives can be arranged over the wrecks - ask at the local restaurants for details or in the dive shops in Fort de France. There is a small museum describing Mount Pelée's terrible eruption, and for the fit a scramble up to the peak of the volcano can be attempted on a clear day. If the weather is bad an alternative excursion to the nearby waterfalls of the Gorges de la Falaise can be spectacular. Mount Pelée and the gorges can be reached by taxi or hired car which are both available in the town. Just south of St Pierre is Anse Turin Bay and the town of Carbet where there is a small museum dedicated to the artist Paul Gauguin who lived there in 1887.

Customs and Immigration

It is possible to enter Martinique at St Pierre, but it is best to do so at Fort de France.

Between St Pierre and the Baie de Fort de France the wind is often light and, when travelling south, it is often necessary to round the Pointe des Nègres before picking up any wind. Strong, sometimes gale force, easterlies occasionally blow out of the Baie de Fort de France. Along this north east coast there are one or two daytime anchorages but nothing of real note. The small private marina at Case Pilote can be entered from the north, leaving the red buoy off the entrance to starboard, but it is usually crowded with local yachts.

The **Baie de Fort de France** is a huge bay in which there are a number of important anchorages. One of the most frequented by visiting yachts is off Fort de France.

Fort de France

The Fort de France anchorage is at the head of the Baie des Flamands. It is a classical anchorage and the gathering place of many transatlantic voyagers from all over the world. Even in the hurricane season there is always a number of yachts at anchor, and throughout the year the anchorage is used by many French charter yachts. The water is murky and the anchorage is often overcrowded, noisy, dirty and subject to an unpleasant swell. Swimming in the Baie des Flamands is not recommended.

Approach

The approach is easy by night or day from any direction. When coming from the north round Pointe des Nègres with its conspicuous lighthouse and pass the apartment blocks in the westerly suburbs of Fort de France. A brown and cream coloured cathedral with a distinctive pointed spire is located in the centre of Fort de France. A shoal extends south from massive Fort St Louis situated at the east end of the town.

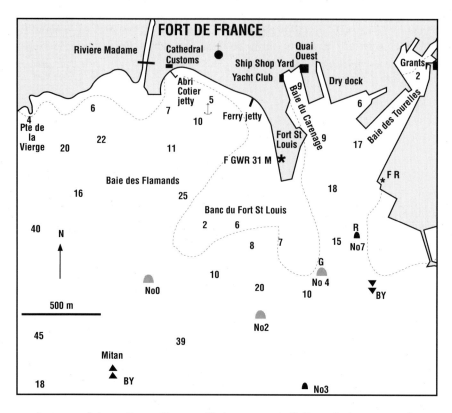

Approaching *from the south* be wary of Cap Solomon where occasional violent offshore squalls swoop down on unwary yachts. If there is a strong easterly blowing out of the Baie de Fort de France hug the sheltered southern shores of the bay before setting out for the anchorage which is east of the complex of tall apartment blocks.

Anchorage

Anchor anywhere off the Abri Cotier jetty in front of an enormous car park and to the west of the central park - La Savane. The holding is good in muddy sand in 5 to 7 metres of cloudy, greenish water. Leave a passage for the ferry boats that run regularly between the docks at the east end of the anchorage and Pointe du Bout.

Alongside and Ashore

Yachts can moor stern-to on the Abri Cotier jetty where there is diesel, ice and water. At the head of the jetty the Abri Cotier office will act as a poste restante (Yacht<>, Poste Restante, L'Abri Cotier, Baie des Flamands, Fort de France, 97200, Martinique, FWI) but it is a service you have to pay for. Abri Cotier also runs a telephone service.

Fort de France anchorage

Leave your dinghy alongside the Abri Cotier jetty or bow-on to a nearby stone wall that lies in front of the car park. Ashore the town is hot, crowded and full of cars, but in or near Fort de France there is almost everything a yacht may require - from a new mast and a diesel engine to a teak swimming ladder. In the town there are two first-class chandleries and a shop specialising in second-hand yacht gear. Just outside the town there is a large industrial estate - the zone industrielle du Lamentin - for those hard to find mechanical spares. It is a good idea to take the broken part with you if you do not speak French. The currency is the French franc. The industrial zone is close to a mooring at Cohe du Lamentin (see below). There are supermarkets galore in Fort de France and at Dillon, just out of town, the excellent Monoprix supermarket.

In Fort de France there is a good, public local/international telephone bureau situated in a side street (Antoine Siger) near the main post office. The main post office is on the west side of the central park (La Savane) on the Rue de la Liberte'. It is often worth using the 'yellow pages' (which are about to become pink) in the telephone book to save time searching for spares, sailmakers etc. You can make local and international calls from the main post office but long queues make it simpler to buy a telephone card and use a street booth. To reverse charges to an international destination from a public phone booth lift the receiver, dial 10 and ask for 'PCV'.

The huge car park in front of the Abri Cotier landing stage is full of 'taxis collectifs' which travel to all parts of Martinique. Their final destinations are painted in the front of the parking lanes as well as being written on the doors of each taxi. Throughout Martinique communal taxis are more frequent than buses, and are about one-tenth the price of normal taxis - which charge Parisian prices. Although communal taxis travel along fixed routes their drivers can sometimes be persuaded to stop or make detours, although this is strictly against the law.

There are frequent ferry services from the jetties at the east end of the Fort de France anchorage to Pointe du Bout marina, Anse Mitan, Anse a l'Ane, Grande Anse and Ste Anne, but some ferry services are seasonal (for example the services to Ste Anne and Grand Anse run only in the summer months).

Fort de France Radio will make link VHF calls to anywhere in the world and they give out an excellent marine weather forecast twice daily on VHF ch 26 at 0730 and 1830 - unfortunately in French. If you miss the forecast they can be persuaded to give it again if you call them on ch16. If you dial 515626 anywhere in Martinique you will obtain a Bulletin Meteo Marine - a recorded weather message in French.

Customs and Immigration

Just by the Abri Cotier landing stage there is a caravan on stilts which houses customs and immigration. This is the main station for yachts entering and clearing Martinique and the office is open every day from 0800 to 1100 and from 1500 to 1700. All the forms are computerised and the service is quick, efficient and, unlike many other places in the Caribbean, there are no overtime charges. It is not possible to live aboard a yacht in any of the French Caribbean islands for longer than six months, unless you wish to import the yacht and pay a tax based upon the estimated value of the boat (the tax is 20% of its value in Martinique, less in Guadeloupe). However, it is possible to leave the yacht uninhabited for periods greater than six months provided the ship's papers are left with the authorities. Inquire at the Abri Cotier custom's caravan for the correct procedure. You will nearly always find the custom officers in Martinique extremely helpful

Just east of the Baie des Flamands anchorage is the Baie du Carenage whose hinterland is almost exclusively dedicated to yacht (and ship) repairs and maintenance.

Baie du Carenage

This is situated below the impressive Fort St Louis. At the head of the bay is the Ship Shop boatyard which has a mobile travel lift capable of lifting yachts displacing up to 40 tons. The entrance to the Baie du Carenage is easy and well buoyed; the only danger is the shoal off Fort St Louis - the Banc du Fort St Louis. Coming from the Baie des Flamands leave the IALA lateral system B ('red right returning') green buoy O off the Banc du Fort St Louis to port, head for the next green buoy 2 and leaving this to port and the red buoys to starboard, enter the bay. As you travel up the bay you will see the private Yacht Club de Martinique on the port bow, but there are no facilities for visiting yachts as all the berths and moorings are filled with local boats.

Ship Shop's yard is in the top right corner of the Baie du Carenage. You can work on your own yacht, and the yard's working facilities are excellent with almost everything to hand - including a high pressure fresh water wash for cleaning the antifouling. The staff are extremely helpful and speak English, but the yard is hot, dirty and buggy and the toilets and showers stink. The east side of the Baie du Carenage is known as Quai Ouest, and here there are a number of extremely useful boat-orientated workshops. If Ship Shop does not have the paint or antifouling you require try Camaco a few hundred yards away where, in addition to selling paint and some chandlery, they test and service liferafts. To the east of Quai Ouest is a big ship dry dock that will take yachts too large for the travel lift. It is much cheaper if you coincide with the dry docking of a number of yachts or a small cargo ship. If your yacht draws around 2 metres you can also haul out on a railway at a nice old fashioned yard, Grants, situated at the head of the next bay east of the Baie du Carenage - the Baie des Tourelles - and now under new management.

All three boatyards are accessible by foot from Fort de France and yachts can anchor in the anchorage in the Baie des Flamands and make arrangements with the yard's manager before hauling out. It is a long hot walk from the Abri Cotier jetty to Grants yard.

East of the Baie des Flamands anchorage off Fort de France and situated in the large Baie de Fort de France are two anchorages and two marinas - all are important hurricane holes. Before approaching these anchorages and marinas first clear Customs and Immigration at Fort de France.

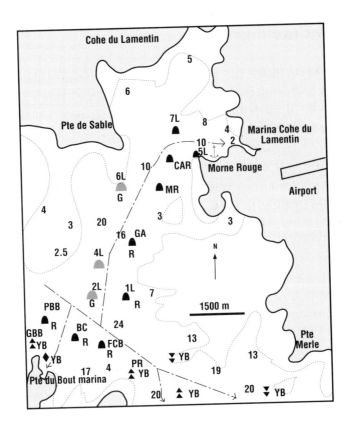

Marina Cohe du Lamentin

The route to this rudimentary marina, or Port Cohe as it is sometimes called, is along a well-buoyed channel that runs up to the marina in the north east corner of the Baie de Fort de France. Yachts coming *from the south or from Pointe du Bout Marina,* should first identify the yellow and black IALA North Cardinal buoy marked GBB not far from Pointe du Bout. Pass north of this buoy if coming from the southwest and head into the channel that is marked with a green, port hand buoy labelled 2L and a red, starboard hand buoy marked 1L. Travel up the channel until the red, starboard hand buoys labelled MR and CAR are passed and then identify the red buoy, 5L, off Pointe de la Vierge. The entrance is through a 1.8 to 2 metres deep dredged channel and 'Port Cohe Marina' is written on a large sign by a wrecked barge near the entrance. As it is safe and sheltered in the marina yachts may be left unattended. Port Cohe is, however, a long way from anywhere - apart from the airport.

Les Trois Ilets

This is a very sheltered region in the south of the Baie de Fort de France and the whole region around the three islands makes an excellent hurricane hole. The Trois Ilets anchorage is best approached from Pointe du Bout. Once off the Pointe pass to the north of the yellow and black North Cardinal buoy marked GBB and head in a south easterly direction to the next yellow and black Cardinal North buoy marked PR and positioned off the Pointe de la Rose. Pass the PR buoy to starboard and head almost directly south to the next point, Pointe Angboeuf. After Angboeuf there are several possible anchorages in depths of 3 to 4 metres in good holding black sticky mud. One is off the golf course near Pointe Galy and is reached by turning to starboard after Pointe Angboeuf. Another is off the town of Trois Ilets, birthplace of Empress Josephine, and reached by keeping Pointe Angboeuf more or less in line with the town jetty, but watch out for the shoals off the island which you will pass to port, before anchoring in a depth of about 2 metres off the town jetty. Another anchorage is behind but not too close to Gros Ilet. Ashore at Trois Ilets there is a small supermarket, a small vegetable market, an interesting church and a couple of restaurants.

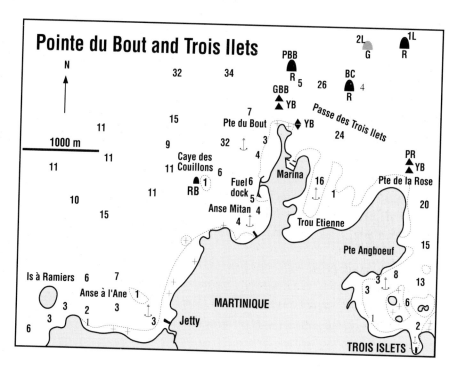

Trou Etienne

The anchorage is situated just east of Pointe du Bout and is a deep water inlet that offers good protection from westerly winds. The anchorage is easy to enter and yachts sometimes move here if, due to a westerly swell, the Anse Mitan anchorage on the west side of Pointe du Bout becomes untenable. Pass north of the yellow and black Cardinal North buoy marked GBB off the end of the Pointe du Bout and to the east of the yellow and black Cardinal East buoy marked B1. The anchorage rapidly shelves from 16 metres to 1 metre.

Pointe du Bout Marina

This is situated about a quarter of a mile south from the tip of Pointe du Bout. It is a well sheltered but airless marina and normally completely full of local yachts and charter boats, but it is occasionally possible, despite the long waiting list, to obtain a berth. First anchor in Anse Mitan (see below) and then come ashore and make arrangements with the Port Captain at the marina. Pointe du Bout is a full service marina and served by a good chandlery (The Captain's Shop, where English is spoken) and a nearby sailmaker (Voilerie Artisanale). A diesel motor shop, marine electronics experts, banks, bars, restaurants, car rentals, discos, night clubs and supermarkets are all close by. The strip of land running back from the marina is one of the most touristic parts of Martinique and there there are numerous holiday flats and small, medium and first class hotels.

Most yachts after entering Martinique at the Baie des Flamands anchorage quickly reprovision in Fort de France and, if they are not hauling out, sail across the Baie de Fort de France and anchor at the much cleaner and calmer anchorage in Anse Mitan.

Because of the many facilities in this region and the proximity of Fort de France, the anchorage in Anse Mitan has become a classical Caribbean anchorage - as many as 100 yachts may be at anchor.

Anse Mitan

This anchorage is often used by French people living aboard their yachts and working in Fort de France or in the marina complex. There is a regular ferry service running between Fort de France and the Pointe du Bout marina.

Approach

From any direction the approach is without difficulty with the only concern being the small shoal - the Caye de l'Anse Mitan (or Caye des Couillons as it is sometimes known, shown on page 75) - that is situated about 150 metres west of the Avimer/Bakoua fuel dock. The fuel dock is about halfway along the narrow strip of land that leads to the Pointe du Bout and just south of the refurbished Bakoua hotel. The shoal has a minimum depth of around 1 metre and is marked by a small unlit white red and black buoy which is often hard to spot as it is surrounded by anchored yachts.

Anchorage

The anchor can be dropped anywhere in this large sandy bay in 3 to 5 metres of water. Do not forget to leave access to the fuel jetty and do not anchor in a 300 metre offshore strip that has to be left for bathers. The anchorage can be uncomfortable in northerly and westerly swells, but if you do not mind the crowd it is breezy and a lot cleaner than the Baie des Flamands.

Alongside and Ashore

Yachts are able to moor stern-to the fuel dock for diesel, petrol, ice and fresh water. On the dock is a supermarket, a bar and a laundry. Drop the anchor off the southern end of the refuelling jetty and power in astern, being careful of the rocks that lie just off the south and east end of the dock. Yachts anchored in the Anse Mitan bay can safely leave their dinghies at the dock; the marina complex, with all its attendant delights, is just a short walk away. Large (20 metres plus) yachts can obtain stern-to berths on the north part of the dock.

Between Cap Solomon and Anse Mitan there are a number of possible anchorages. Probably the best is at **Anse à l'Ane** (see page 75), but beware of the unmarked 1.3 metre shoal in the middle of the bay. When travelling to Anse a`l'Ane from Anse Mitan give the rocks off Pointe d'Alet a wide berth as you travel down the coast, to anchor in a depth of about 3 metres in good holding sand. There is an occasional ferry to Fort de France from the jetty and there are restaurants ashore and a clean beach from which to swim. There are anchorages in settled conditions east and south west of the Ilet à Ramiers and daytime anchorages in the beautiful bays of **Anse Noire** and **Anse Dufour**.

Grande Anse d'Arlet

Situated on the south west coast of Martinique under Cap Solomon in a beautiful golden-sanded bay, Grande Anse d'Arlet is a truly classical Caribbean anchorage. But, it is often crowded at weekends with local yachts and power boats from Fort de France and the Pointe du Bout Marina.

Approach
By day and from any direction the approach is straightforward. Both headlands are steep-to and there are no offlying dangers. It is forbidden to anchor in the middle of the bay in the area marked by the unlit yellow buoys. This region is kept clear for seine net fishing and the summertime ferry that runs to and from Fort de France from the dock in the middle of the bay. Anchor either in the north or south of the bay - the best, most sheltered anchorage is in the south east corner.

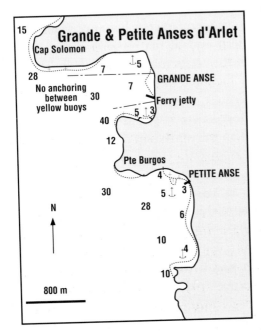

Anchorage
Drop the anchor anywhere in depths between 3 and 7 metres - the bottom shelves gradually. Catamarans and shallow draft yachts anchor almost on the beach.

Ashore
In the small village you will find two supermarkets - one at the north end of the village and one just along the road towards Petite Anse d'Arlet, and a good selection of bars and restaurants. There is good

snorkelling off both headlands and a wonderful walk to Morne Champagne. Follow the marked path out of Grande Anse and up to the southern headland to an abandoned cottage, complete with its own fresh water pond and water lilies - it could be the south of England.

Petite Anse d'Arlet

The next bay south has a picturesque fishing village with a beautiful wooden church. Petite Anse has remained almost unchanged since the days of sail. The Martiniquan traditional fishing boats, the brightly painted 'gommiers', bring a wealth of contrasting colours to the golden sand of the beach. Many still carry sails in case their powerful outboard motors let them down in the passage between Martinique and Saint Lucia. The fishermen are keen participants in the 'Round the Island' sailing gommier race in early August.

Approach
This presents no problem by day. Head either for the north or south corners of the bay. If aiming for the north corner watch out for a collection of rocks, some of them exposed, situated just north of the jetty in the middle of the bay. The jetty runs out into the sea in front of a conspicuous church that is in the middle of the village.

Anchorage
Anchor in either the north or south parts of the bay in good holding sand in 3 to 7 metre depths. The anchorages in this bay are sometimes exposed to the Atlantic swell and, because of the roll, they can become uncomfortable.

Ashore
The village has a post office, bars, restaurants, shops, a library, and a twice weekly cinema.

In the south of Martinique are two classical anchorages, one off the village of Sainte Anne and the other in the nearby, well-protected Cul de Sac du Marin. The Cul de Sac du Marin is one of the best hurricane holes in the Caribbean, but to sail there from the west coast of Martinique can be an eight hour up-wind slog against the trade winds, a swell and two knots of contrary current. It is not unknown for yachts to tack almost across the channel to Saint Lucia before they are able to lay the approach to either the Cul de Sac du Marin or the anchorage off Sainte Anne. Yachts sailing north to either of these two anchorages from St Lucia will usually have a comfortable reach. (Make sure that you enter Martinique at the custom station at Marin, before anchoring off Sainte Anne, if you have come from Saint Lucia.)

Off the south west corner of Martinique is a distinctive landmark for yachts approaching southern Martinique from any direction - the Rocher du Diamant (Diamond Rock). This 178.9 metres high rock is steep-to and was once taken and fortified by the British during the Napoleonic Wars. Under calm conditions there is a difficult anchorage in a depth of about 12 metres under its lee. From this anchorage it is almost impossible to imagine how the British sailors landed and hauled their cannons and supplies to the top of this almost sheer-faced rock. For months they harassed the French ships trying to put into Fort de France. The British sailors lived in caves and repulsed a number of attempts to retake the rock, but they eventually succumbed to the French and liquor; before mounting their final assault the French cunningly floated barrels of rum down on to the rock.

Off the southern coast of Martinique, Diamond Rock to port.

Cul de Sac du Marin

Cul de Sac du Marin is a two mile long, extremely well sheltered bay that is surrounded by mangrove trees. At the head of the Cul de Sac is the town of Marin which has a municipal quay, a yacht club, a customs office and ATM Yachts, one of the largest charter companies in the Caribbean.

Approach

Overlooking the entrance channel to the Cul de Sac du Marin, the Passe du Marin, is a conspicuous landmark - 274 metres high Morne Aca which has a television pylon on its summit. The Passe du Marin channel is easy by day and just possible by night - but do not be tempted to cut corners as there are a number of dangerous reefs off the Passe. Do not try to enter at night on your first visit, and remember that there is a good chance, as for anywhere else in the Caribbean, that buoys and sectored lights may not be lit.

Identify the green buoy off Pointe Borgnesse, marked MA2 in large white letters, and leave it to port. The next buoy is red, marked MA1, and when entering is left to starboard. Both buoys are unlit, but the next green port hand buoy MA4 that marks the southern end of the dangerous Banc du Singe is lit (Fl (2) G 5s). Just before the end of the Pointe Marin is a sectored light (Q WRG 7M) and its white sector covers the safe passage through the Passe du Marin. This light is just south of a lit, 5 metres high, red beacon (Fl R 2s 2M) that is situated at the tip of Pointe Marin.

A Club Med complex has been built on Pointe Marin, so when entering watch out for tumbling water skiers, small sailing dinghies and windsurfers, as you leave the red beacon on Pointe Marin to starboard. Head in a north easterly direction towards two lit beacons and leave the green beacon (Fl (2) G 5s) to port and the red beacon (Fl R 2s) to starboard.

If your destination is the municipal quay off the town of Marin identify the town cemetery that lies behind and to the east of a black and yellow Cardinal East buoy. Pass the Cardinal East beacon to port and drop the anchor in depths of 4 to 5 metres in good-holding black sticky mud.

If heading towards the Club Nautique or the ATM charter yacht quay identify two green painted beacons and four red buoys. The beacons are lit - the most westerly beacon has the shorter cycle (Fl (3)

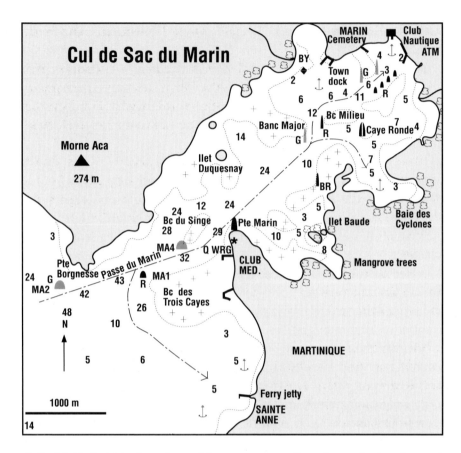

G 5s: Fl (3) G 10s) - but the red buoys are not. Pass through the channel marked by the beacons and buoys, leaving the beacons on the port bow and the red buoys to starboard.

Anchorage

The most popular anchorage in the Cul de Sac du Marin is just south of the two green beacons in depths around 6 metres of water and a bottom of good-holding sticky black mud. When anchoring near the two green beacons make sure you keep clear of the fixed moorings that are usually filled with charter and local boats, and do not block the passage through to the ATM charter yacht quays. The anchorage can become very busy with ATM charter yacht leaving and returning at high speed.

Alongside and Ashore

If you wish to go alongside it is possible to moor bow-on to the visitor berth on the Club Nautique quay which is north of ATM charter yachts and marked 'Quai d'Accueil'. There is electricity and fresh water on the quay.

The Quai d'Accueil is often full so it is best first to anchor off and take the dinghy ashore to check out the quay. Make arrangements to go alongside at the Club Nautique, which is the large building on the beach. There is a restaurant and bar over the Club Nautique and scuba diving can be arranged from the Club.

In Marin village there are good supermarkets, some small restaurants, a sail maker, a post office, a bank, fresh vegetables from a market and street vendors and garages with batteries for sale. Collective taxis run regularly to Fort de France (about FF 25).

Customs and Immigration

The Marin customs post is situated on the waterfront by the town dock. The officials speak little English but they are extremely helpful and the office is open most days.

The Cul de Sac du Marin is probably one of the safest refuges in the Caribbean during a hurricane. Perhaps the best hurricane hole in the Cul de Sac is in the Baie des Cyclones. To enter the bay turn to starboard just before the red and green beacons. On the port bow there is a black and red beacon (marking the Caye Ronde) and leaving this to port enter the Baie des Cyclones. Drop your anchors and tie up to the mangroves.

Sainte Anne

South of Cul de Sac du Marin, about a mile south of the Club Med and Pointe Marin, is the Mouillage de Ste Anne, a classical Caribbean anchorage off the small seaside town of Sainte Anne.

Approach

From a westerly direction the approach is easy during the day or night. When coming from Marin do not turn to port until you have passed buoy MA1. The coral reefs marked by this buoy at Caye Beau and Banc des Trois Cayes have damaged many keels and holed a few of my friends' boats. Off Ste Anne the sea is heavily fished and everywhere there are fishing traps with tiny white propellor-grabbing floats so take great care.

Anchorage

Anchor anywhere off the town of Sainte Anne in a gently-shelving sandy bottom in depths between 3 and 6 metres. There is a town dock where you can safely leave the dinghy. It is much used by ferries that travel to Fort de France in the summer time and an 'aquascope' that offers daily trips to Pointe Borgnesse. Yachts can anchor off the beach that leads from Sainte Anne to the Club Med but only outside the yellow buoys which cordon off a large area that is reserved for bathers and watersports.

Ashore

In the town there are two good supermarkets, a post office with telephones, a number of bars, boutiques, scooter hire and restaurants.

There are anchorages on the east, windward coast of Martinique and a small marina at Robert, but the entrance to all of them is difficult and they should only be approached with local knowledge. A number of yachts have recently been lost off the east coast.

The Ste Anne anchorage and the entrance to Cul de Sac du Marin

Martinique-Saint Lucia Channel

This 18-mile channel that separates Martinique and Saint Lucia is a comfortable day sail. The current is west going, sometimes north west, and varies from negligible to up to two knots. The sail to Rodney Bay, the classical anchorage in northern Saint Lucia, from Sainte Anne in Martinique (and vice versa) is usually a reach, as is the sail from Fort de France to Rodney Bay.

Charts
French: 7041 North, 6738 South, 6892 Baie de Fort de France, 7089 Details
British Admiralty: 371 General, 494 Details
USA: 25524 General, 25527 Baie de Fort de France
Imray Iolaire: A30 General and Details

Radio Station, Frequency and Times of Weather Bulletin
RFO:1310 kHz (0630,1259,1930)
RCL: 840 kHz
VHF 26: 0730,1830 (after a general call on ch 16)

Airport
An international airport (Aeroport International du Lamentin) at Lamentin is about a 20-minute drive from Fort de France. Taxis run regularly from La Savane area, but unfortunately the cheaper collective taxis do not stop at the airport. Tel: 515151

SAINT LUCIA

Saint Lucia was sighted in 1502 during Columbus' fourth and last voyage to the Caribbean when, after 21 days at sea, he made a landfall on Martinique. Although the Europeans had arrived in this part of the Caribbean, for the next 150 years the Caribs retained their stronghold on Saint Lucia as the high mountains and thick tropical rain forests gave them excellent protection and hindered any would-be colonisers. They destroyed an attempted English settlement in 1639 and later formed a pact with the French. The French were often quite successful in combining forces with the Caribs against the English but Saint Lucia was too close to the important French island of Martinique to be left alone by the British, and the Caribs were finally subdued. Throughout the eighteenth and early nineteenth centuries Britain and France fought desperately for the control of strategically important Saint Lucia and the island changed hands 14 times before it finally became a British colony in 1814. Saint Lucia became a Commonwealth state in 1967 and obtained full independence in 1979. Today there are about 124 000 inhabitants of mostly African descent. The capital Castries, once an important British Empire coaling station, has a population of around 45 000.

Beautiful, lush and one of the largest of the Windward Islands, Saint Lucia is crossed by deep gorges and ravines and dominated by high peaks. There are many sheltered bays and miles of golden-sanded beaches, and as a result Saint Lucia has successfully expanded its tourist industry. There is an 'island hopping' short runway airport at Vigie Field close to Castries, a new passenger ship terminal in Castries Harbour, an international airport at Hewanorra in the south of the island, and near this airport a French-owned Club Med. The Americans had a large airbase near Vieux Fort in the south of the island during World War II and recently they have invested heavily in two major yachting developments - one at Rodney Bay and the other at Marigot Bay.

Rodney Bay is usually the first stop for yachts voyaging south from Martinique. It is a large bay situated in the north west of Saint Lucia with at least two good anchorages. Connected to the bay by a dredged channel are two lagoons - the outer lagoon contains a full service marina and the inner lagoon makes a reasonable hurricane hole.

Rodney Bay

Approach

The entrance to Rodney Bay from any direction is easy by day, and possible by night, but do not try to enter the dredged channel to the lagoons at night. By day or night beware of the dozens of tiny, white fishing trap floats that are found all over the bay. When *approaching from Martinique*, as soon as Saint Lucia comes into view, steer for the highest northern mountain. As you close the leeward side of the island identify Burgot Rocks which stand out from steeply rising Pigeon Island.

The fort, hospital and barracks on Pigeon Island in the north of Rodney Bay were once an important part of the British Navy's presence in the West Indies; now they are in ruins. Pigeon Island is not a true island but is connected to the mainland by a narrow strip of sand. As you approach Pigeon Island the palm covered 'causeway' that connects it to the mainland is a good landmark. Yachts can anchor behind the island but they should have entered Saint Lucia first - there is a Customs and Immigration post in Rodney Bay Marina.

Approaching Rodney Bay *from a southerly direction* after passing Port Castries keep clear of Rat Island before entering the bay. Pass either side of Barrel of Beef Rock which is supposed to be lit (FL (2) 5s) but the light rarely works.

Pigeon Island

The anchorage is behind the island and well protected. Drop the anchor south east of the island and some distance away from the sand causeway in depths of about 4 metres in good holding sand. There is a little stone dock for the dinghy. The climb up to the old naval base and its well-kept gardens is a must.

Reduit Bay

Anchor in hard sand in depths between 4 and 7 metres anywhere between the Saint Lucian Hotel and the entrance to the lagoons and Rodney Bay Marina. The water is not very clear and there are occasional small rocks on the sea bed so make sure you set the anchor well in by going hard astern on the motor.

Rodney Bay lagoons

The entrance to the outer and inner lagoons is through a dredged 3 metres deep channel in the centre of Rodney Bay. The entrance is marked with small red and green beacons which are sometimes lit. It is possible to anchor and moor stern-to at the A Frame dock which is situated in the inner lagoon and is much cheaper than the marina. There is water and electricity (and the berth is very close to the A Frame's bar!) but it is hot, buggy and airless in this part of the inner lagoon.

Rodney Bay Marina

The marina is one of the best equipped and most attractive marinas in the Windward Islands. There are 140 side tie berths that can take yachts drawing up to 3 metres and over 20 metres long. On the north side of the outer lagoon there is the Marina's boatyard where there is long-term dry storage, an excellent paint and materials store, machine, wood and engineering workshops and a 50-ton mobile lift. You can work on your own boat or hire labour. In front of the yard there is a fuel dock that sells diesel, ice and water. There are telephones, a fax and telex near the marina office.

Alongside and Ashore
The west pontoons are for visiting yachts (the inside pontoons are reserved for charter yachts) and all the berths have electricity and water.

Admiralty
Bay, Bequia

Diamond Rock from afar

Across the bay from the fishing settlement in Friendship Bay, Bequia

The Two Pitons, St Lucia

The morning catch Ensa
Esmeralda, Venezuela

Carenage, St George's, Grenada

Gommiers ashore at Anse
d'Arlet, Martinique

Tobago Cays in
the rainy season

Iles des Saintes.
Guadeloupe in
the distance

Anse du Bourg,
Iles des Saintes

Marigot Bay, looking seaward, St Lucia

The church from the jetty at Petite Anse d'Arlet, Martinique

The Gosier anchorage, Guadeloupe

Round the Island Race, Martinique

A new schooner, Tyrell Bay, Carriacou

Kingstown tenements, St Vincent

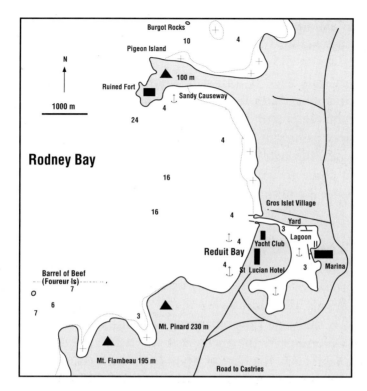

Very large yachts moor on the end pontoons. In the marina complex there is a marine electronics shop, a sail loft, a laundry, a fresh water swimming pool, a chandlery, bars and restaurants, small supermarkets and hot and cold showers.

Once moored alongside you can take the dinghy and visit the bars and restaurants that are clustered around the inner lagoon: Charthouse, Giogios, A Frame and the Mortar and Pestle on the water's edge, and Sweet Dreams, The Lime, Rib Shack and Capones behind the St Lucian Hotel, as well as Eagle's Inn on the south side of the dredged entrance channel. The anchorage off Reduit Beach offers sophisticated entertainment, boutiques, and the bars and restaurants of the St Lucian Hotel. On Friday nights there is a wild 'jump up' in the streets at Gros Islet Village on the north side of the lagoon and about a half an hour walk from the marina. If you are walking (but there are plenty of taxis) it is better to travel in a group as there have been some reports of petty robberies.

Castries, which was named after an eighteenth-century French naval minister Maréchal de Castries, is only a dollar EC bus ride away. Flag down the bus from the roadside opposite the marina entrance and be prepared for a noisy, hair-raising ride.

Customs and Immigration

Rodney Bay Marina is a good place to enter and clear Saint Lucia. The office faces out over the pontoons and if you are taking a marina berth just walk over. If you wish to anchor off in Rodney Bay you should first enter Saint Lucia either by bringing your yacht into the marina and temporarily mooring to the yellow posted customs berths on the west pontoons and visiting the offices or, if your yacht is too large to pass through the dredged channel, anchor off outside in the bay and come in with the ship's papers by dinghy. There is an overtime fee if you enter or clear from 1630 - 1830 and on Saturdays.

Vigie and Castries

South of Rodney Bay is the large well-sheltered port of Castries, and tucked away in the north side of the bay, that leads up to the town of Castries, is the Vigie Cove anchorage and the nearby Castries Yacht Centre. Unfortunately the anchorages off Castries are dirty. If you are entering Saint Lucia you have to report to the Customs jetty at the town quay. If the customs' berth is occupied you must drop anchor by the customs buoy. There are heavy fines for yachts which do not carry out these instructions.

Approach

The entrance to Port Castries is easy by day and possible by night. The Vigie lighthouse (Fl(2) 10s 24M) situated behind Pointe d'Estrees is a good landmark. When *coming from the north*, yachts can round Pointe d'Estrees fairly close-to and identify the sunken barge off the end of the Vigie Field runway which is marked with a green beacon (Q G).

From the south give the lit Tapion rock (Q) a good clearance before turning to starboard and leave the red buoy (Q R) to starboard. There are two leading lights that show fixed red (F R) and line up on 121° True.

Anchorage

Pass the Castries Yacht Centre and anchor in depths of about 4 metres in the entrance to Vigie Cove. The entrance to the cove is just before the new passenger ship terminal at Pointe Seraphine where there are distinctive red roofed buildings which are a part of the tax-free shopping complex. At the head of Vigie Creek is the almost-defunct Saint Lucia Yacht Services where at the broken-down fuel dock (least

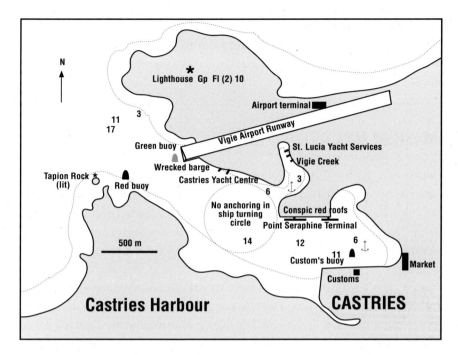

N

Lighthouse Gp Fl (2) 10

Airport terminal

11
17   3

Vigie Airport Runway

Green buoy

St. Lucia Yacht Services

Vigie Creek

Tapion Rock (lit)

Wrecked barge

Castries Yacht Centre   3

Red buoy

6

No anchoring in
ship turning
circle

Conspic red roofs

Point Seraphine Terminal

500 m   14   12   6

Custom's buoy   11

Market

Customs

Castries Harbour   **CASTRIES**

depth 2.5 metres) you can obtain diesel and fresh water. A seafood
restaurant is next to the docks.

Alongside and Ashore

Yachts can haul out at Castries Yacht Centre which can be
contacted on VHF ch16 and has a 35-ton travel lift. The Centre is
surrounded by a strong fence and has full 24-hour security so that
yachts can be safely dry stored in the yard. There are hot showers, a
fuel dock, fresh water, fibreglass repair facilities, tool rentals, a
machine shop, a full range of topside paints and antifoulings, and
the English manager is very helpful. But the yard is close to the
noisy airport, is some distance from Castries and there are no local
food shops.

Castries was burnt down in 1948 but parts of the town still have a
certain charm, especially around Columbus Square. Castries has an
excellent daily cheap vegetable market, a covered-in market which is
worth visiting, hospitals, telephones and a post office, banks and
supermarkets but little to offer in the way of yacht chandlery. The
vast duty free shopping complex at Pointe Seraphine was
constructed for visiting passenger ships but it is also available to
visiting yachts, providing you take passports and the ship's papers
along with you when you visit.

Customs and Immigration

Entering yachts have to moor alongside the customs dock or be fined (see above). It is better to enter and clear Saint Lucia from either Rodney or Marigot Bays.

Marigot Bay

South of Castries and about a mile from the enormous tanker and oil storage depot at Cul de Sac Bay is the famous Caribbean anchorage of Marigot Bay. A calm, sheltered lagoon, half hidden behind tall, elegant palm trees, with romantic candle-lit dining in restaurants on the water's edge and swimming from golden-sanded beaches - Marigot Bay is the holiday brochure picture of Caribbean yachting. But the anchorage is airless, the mosquitoes persistent, the water murky and the charter boats packed and noisy. The anchorage might be a useful hurricane hole, but only if you can find room in the mangroves amongst the dozens of charter boats and if the wind and seas are from the west.

Approach

The entrance to Marigot Bay is well hidden, but the nearby oil storage tanks of Cul de Sac Bay are good landmarks for approaches from any direction. It is best to enter by day and a second good landmark is a conspicuous red roofed house high on the hill of the southern headland. Keep to the south side of the outer bay when entering.

Anchorage

It is possible to drop the anchor in the outer bay, but it is deep - 8 to 12 metres. Most yachts pass the sand spit that protects the inner bay and anchor in 5 metres of cloudy, yellow water in thick black mud. Do not anchor on the cable that runs across the entrance to the inner bay.

Alongside and Ashore

The American charter company, The Moorings, runs two good hotels/restaurants/ bars - Dolittles and the Hurricane Hole Hotel - as well as the 40 or so charter boats that work out of the bay. The Hurricane Hole has a small fresh water swimming pool and a games room. The Moorings manager will give assistance to cruising yachts with problems but, of course, the company's boats take preference. The Moorings own the marina, the fuel and water dock, and the new

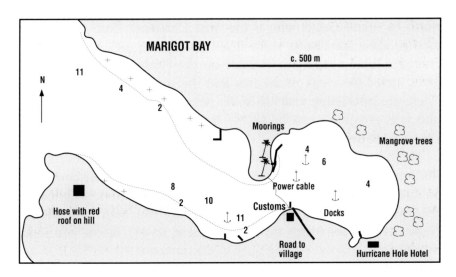

supermarket. The company also operates a free ferry service between the two hotels and the road. A local shop is situated in the village of Marigot which is at the top of the road which winds up a steep hill. In the village there is a good local restaurant (JJs) and a few bars. A fairly cheap restaurant (Odins) has recently opened on the south side of the outer bay. There are taxis to Castries or, if you walk past the village and down to the main road, you can catch a bus.

Customs and Immigration
The office is situated on the south side of the inner bay just to the west of the road that leads up to the village. You can enter and clear Saint Lucia from here.

About three miles south of Marigot Bay is a delightful anchorage in the north east corner of **Anse Cochon** bay, which opens after you have passed a rock covered headland. The quiet of this lonely anchorage is now often spoilt as day hire charter boats from Marigot Bay have recently discovered it. South of Anse Cochon there is nothing until the anchorages in Soufrière Bay.

Hummingbird Restaurant, Soufrière Bay

Soufrière Bay lies between Grand Caille Point and Beaumont Point and on the shores of this huge deep bay are two of the Caribbean's most famous mountains - the Two Pitons. There is much to do and see. Just north of Grand Caille Point is the Anse Chastanet Hotel which will arrange some spectacular scuba dives down sheer rock walls. For the energetic hiker a six hour scramble up the Pitons with a local guide gives incredible views of the bay and the surrounding countryside. There are interesting visits to some nearby molten Sulphur Springs and it is possible to bathe in the hot water springs that feed the Diamond Baths.

The best anchorage in Soufrière Bay is off the Hummingbird Restaurant. The restaurant is situated in the north east corner of Soufrieѐ Bay. As you approach the anchorage you will be accosted by the boat loads of local boys all vying to take your stern line ashore. Negotiate the fee, which should be around $5 EC, before you send out the line.

Approach
From the south there are no problems by day. Approaching *from the north* make sure you keep clear of the reefs that extend some 200 metres offshore from Grand Caille Point and just south of the Anse Chastanet Hotel. Turn to port and the Hummingbird Restaurant anchorage (they stand by on VHF ch 16) is tucked away in the north east corner.

Anchorage
The water is very deep everywhere in Soufrière Bay. Drop the anchor in depths of 20 to 25 metres (so you need a good anchor winch if you use only chain). Approach the shore stern first, letting out the anchor chain or line as you go. Have a long stern warp ready which the boat boys will take and pass round a coconut tree and, if the line is long enough, return to you.

Alongside and Ashore
At the Hummingbird Restaurant there is a bar, a first class restaurant, a dinghy dock and a sandy beach that is kept illuminated throughout the night. You can obtain taxis from the restaurant for trips to the town of Soufrière, the Two Pitons (Petit Piton and Gros Piton) that rise dramatically over 600 metres out of the sea, the Sulphur Springs and Diamond Baths.

A second anchorage in Soufrière Bay is off the town of Soufrière, Saint Lucia's second largest town. Drop the anchor off the quay in about 10 metres. The town is poor, the water deep, the boat boys can be very persistent and there have been a number of thefts from yachts moored in this region, so do not leave your boat unattended. A much better anchorage is off the Two Pitons.

Two Pitons

An incredibly scenic but isolated anchorage lies at the foot of the Two Pitons.

Approach
The anchorage actually lies below Petit Piton. When coming *from the south*, round Beaumont Point and head for Petit Piton. Everywhere in the bay the water is very deep. Close the shore and head for the anchorage under Petit Piton in front of the cluster of palm trees.

Anchorage
Drop anchor in depths of 20 to 25 metres and send a line ashore to a coconut tree.

Ashore
Nothing except an elephant that belongs to a nearby hotel!

Vieux Fort

Vieux Fort is off the popular sailing route and a tough beat against the trade winds and Atlantic swell, but when you arrive it is a well sheltered haven. The fishing is usually very good along this part of the coast so do not forget to trail a line if you want tuna for supper! Yachts sailing to Saint Vincent from Vieux Fort have an easier sail than if their point of departure from Saint Lucia is Point Beaumont below Gros Piton.

Approach
From the west coast of Saint Lucia round Beaumont Point and be prepared for a tough first half hour as you struggle against wind and tide. You could be beating into at least one and half knots of north west-going current. Keep away from the reef that extends about half a mile from the shor between Chiseul and Laborie.

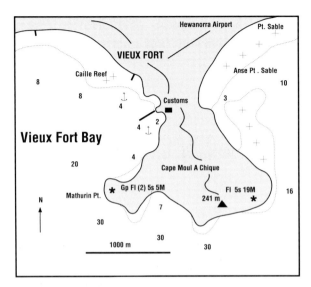

Anchorage
The anchorage is south of the large concrete cargo ship jetty or by the ruins of the old wooden town jetty beneath the Kimatri Hotel south of Caille Reef. A large generator runs all night by the cargo ship dock so a quieter anchorage is over nearer the town.

Ashore
Vieux Fort is an attractive town with basic shops and a few hotels.

Customs and Immigration
Vieux Fort is a port of entry and customs and immigration are located just off the large cargo dock.

When sailing from Saint Lucia to the Grenadines many yachts choose to anchor at Marigot Bay and leave just before dawn. They generally sail directly to Bequia Island without stopping, but there are a few anchorages off Saint Vincent that are worth considering.

Charts
British Admiralty: 1273 General, 499 Details
French: 4985 General
USA: 25521 General, 25528 Details
Imray Iolaire: B1 General

Radio Station, Frequency and Times of Weather Bulletins
Radio St Lucia: 625/660 kHz
Radio Caribbean: 550/840 kHz

Airports
Hewanorra International Airport is close to Vieux Fort. Tel: 4546355.
Inter-island Airport is not far from Castries.

SAINT VINCENT

The island of Saint Vincent was so named as Columbus first saw it on Saint Vincent's day in 1498 on his third voyage to the Caribbean. Had he landed he would have found a wild, mountainous country inhabited by the Caribs. The Caribs called their land 'Hairoon' - home of the blessed - and they had complete control of the island until the middle of the eighteenth century, when the colonial wars between France and England encompassed Saint Vincent. England obtained a foothold on the island in 1763 but it was lost to France during the American Revolution. The 1783 Treaty of Versailles returned Saint Vincent to Britain.

Meanwhile another force, hostile to Britain, had been developing within the island. A slave ship was wrecked off Saint Vincent's coast in 1675 and the Africans were immediately taken as slaves by the Caribs, but these Africans were from a fierce and independent tribe, and turning on their captors they escaped into the tropical forests taking with them a number of Carib women. These Africans prospered and, adopting the Carib way of life, became known as 'Black Caribs', eventually taking over the island from the Amerindian Caribs. The Black Caribs settled in the north of Saint Vincent, leaving the south to the British settlers. France joined forces with the Black Caribs and fostered a rebellion but, in 1795, this alliance was defeated by a powerful British force and 5 000 Black Caribs were deported to Honduras.

Saint Vincent remained a British colony until it became fully independent in 1979, the same year that a 1219-metre high volcano, Soufrière, erupted. Previously Soufrière had erupted in 1902 killing some 30 000 people, just two days before Mount Pelée exploded in Martinique and destroyed the town of St Pierre. Soufrière erupted again in 1973 and, although there there were no casualties, the lava streams still scar the island's northern slopes. The volcano rises high over the north of the island, its top nearly always shrouded in cloud, and behind the clouds the volcano appears to be simmering. It has a majestic, looming presence and the dark grey frozen lava streams that once cut their way through the tropical forests are a continuous reminder of the volcano's massive but dormant power.

The passage between Saint Lucia and Saint Vincent can be a comfortable broad reach or a windy rough beat - it usually depends on the time of year. When travelling south from Saint Lucia in the winter months you will often have a reach as the wind is more northerly than in the summer months. It is best to keep close to Beaumont Point before heading out into the channel and, if in doubt about the conditions, double reef the main before you leave Beaumont Point as the wind round the southern end of Saint Lucia can be strong and the seas steep and confused. A few miles clear of the island the seas will calm a little and the wind will drop - then you can remove the reefs at leisure. Likewise, when coming north to Saint Lucia from Saint Vincent, keep close to De Volet Point and double reef the main before heading out into the channel; wind and seas are often worse here than off Beaumont Point. You sometimes see bareboat charter yachts turning back as they experience the bad conditions off these headlands, but persevere as the conditions will improve as you continue into the passage.

There are few anchorages on the west coast of Saint Vincent, and none are especially good. Many yachts voyaging south from Saint Lucia leave Marigot Bay very early in the morning and head for Bequia without stopping at Saint Vincent since it is a lot easier to enter (and clear) Saint Vincent and the Grenadines from Bequia than from the capital Kingstown, which is Saint Vincent's deep water port in the south of the island. Some yachts stop at Soufrière or the Pitons on Saint Lucia and head for Cumberland or Wallilabou Bay on Saint Vincent. When in a hurry I head straight for Bequia.

Travelling down the west coast there is plenty of water close to the island and the only danger not cleared by keeping about a quarter of a mile offshore is the Bottle and Glass reef which is about half way along Saint Vincent. There is an anchorage in **Chateaubelair Bay** south of Point Richmond where there are two distinctive radio masts. Enter Chateaubelair Bay and anchor in deep water off the village and between the Fitzhughe's Estates. There is a slightly better anchorage off the fishing village of **Petit Bordel**, and it is possible to sail there through the passage between Chateaubelair Island and the mainland. South of Dark Head is Cumberland Bay, a black-sanded, deep water bay.

Cumberland Bay

The entrance to Cumberland Bay is hard to find but the boat boys will probably have accosted you at least a mile from the entrance - and asked for a tow back to the bay. It is about a mile south of Dark Head which has a light (Fl 5s 338 ft 12M).

Approach
There is a rocky shoal off the southern headland so keep to the north of the bay.

Anchorage
The water is very deep, coming up quickly from 40 to 10 metres , and the shelf is narrow. Anchor close to the shore in hard black sand. The boat lads will, for about $5 EC, take a stern line ashore to a convenient coconut tree. Alternatively you could drop a stern anchor and pass a bow line ashore. There have been thefts from yachts in Cumberland Bay and Wallilabou (or Wallilabu) Bay so always keep someone on board, and use an old rope for the stern line as they have been known to go missing during the night!

Ashore
Stephens' Hideaway restaurant is just up the hill and serves local food at a reasonable price. Call the restaurant on VHF ch 16 and Mr Stephens will send a car down for you and leave someone to keep an eye on your boat. There is a fresh water stream running in to the north east corner of Cumberland Bay.

Wallilabou Bay

This bay is about a mile south of Cumberland and again the boat boys will have picked you up long before you arrive. Like Cumberland Bay, Wallilabou is deep and black-sanded and the shelf is narrow. There is

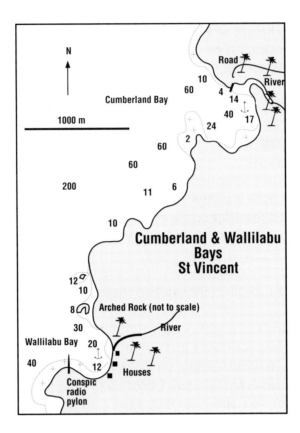

a small collection of houses in the south part of the bay and a river enters its north east corner.

Approach
From the north there is a conspicuous rock arch off the the north headland. On the southern headland a radio pylon (incorrectly positioned on British Admiralty chart 791) is a distinctive landmark.

Anchorage
Anchor as close to the beach as possible and send a stern line ashore to the coconut trees. There have been thefts from yachts so be vigilant.

Ashore
There is a batik shop, a refreshing fresh water waterfall ten minutes walk up the road, and a bus service to Kingstown.

At Fort Charlotte on Johnson Point there is supposedly a powerful light (Gp Fl (3) 20s 640ft 33M). I have seen yachts anchored in the south of York Bay and in the next bay south, Ottley Hall Bay.

Customs and Immigration

Before you anchor in any of these west coast anchorages you should have first entered Saint Vincent at Union, Bequia (see below) or Kingstown. However, recently the authorities are taking a more relaxed attitude to yachts anchoring without first having entered.

Kingstown Bay

Kingstown, the island's capital and the port of entry, is at the head of Kingstown Bay. Saint Vincent has around 105 000 inhabitants, 23 000 of which live in Kingstown which is a busy port and offers only a poor anchorage for the cruising yacht. The best spot is to the east of the ferry dock, but the water is filthy, there can be an unpleasant swell and the quayside lads can be a real nuisance - never leave the dinghy or the yacht unattended. The customs office is just off the cargo ship dock (open 0800 - 1200 and 1400 - 1600) and immigration is about a ten minute walk away west along Bay Street. Parts of the town, especially around the Cobblestone Inn, are interesting and there are supermarkets, a vegetable market, some yacht chandlery at Gunn's and St Vincent Sales and Services - but overall the town is poor and depressing. It is best to visit Kingstown by ferry from Bequia or by road from Young Island Cut or the Blue Lagoon.

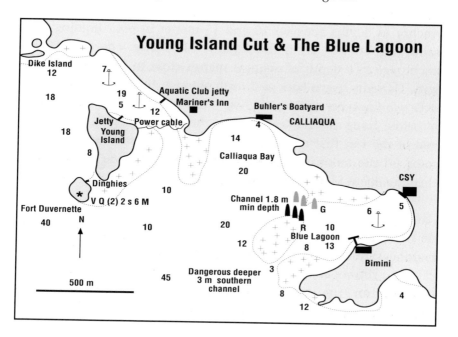

Young Island Cut

This is a good anchorage for the airport, but there have been thefts from yachts anchored in the Young Island Cut and nearby Blue Lagoon.

Approach

Approach always *from the west*. There are strong one to two knot westerly currents that flow along the south coast of Saint Vincent, and tide rips can occur off Johnson Point and Cane Garden Point. Give Washing Rock a clear berth south of Cane Garden Point. The approach to Young Island Cut is easy by day; head for the shore east of Dike Island and north of Young Island towards the broken-down jetty by the Aquatic Club. Do not try to enter Young Island Cut from the east as the channel is much narrower, and dangerous shoals extend from the east side of Young Island.

When approaching the Cut *from Bequia* it is best to motor sail along Bequia's north coast to somewhere around Anse du Chemin before making the passage across to the Cut. If the seas are rough off the north coast, and they can be very steep, give up the fight and sail your best course to anywhere on Saint Vincent. Then work your way along the south coast to approach the Cut from the west.

Anchorage

Anchor in depths between 10 and 15 metres in poor holding hard sand. A good spot is off the Aquatic Club jetty. There is also an anchorage in a depth of about 8 metres close to the Young Island jetty. Currents sweep back and forth through the Cut, sometimes at over two knots, so use two anchors and make sure they are well dug in before going ashore. Keep clear of the electric cable at the eastern end of the Cut that connects the island to the mainland. Recently some private mooring buoys have been laid and you can moor to them for about $10 EC a night.

Ashore

At Young Island Cut, by the Aquatic Club jetty, there is a range of boutiques, restaurants and bars - the Mariners Inn, The Dolphin (you can get a shower at both these places), the French Restaurant and the Mermaid Inn. The Scuba Shop and Dive St Vincent organise scuba diving at sites off St Vincent as well as the Grenadines. On Young

Island there is a first class resort where you can dine or just take the sunset cocktail. Just south of Young Island is Duvernette Island and the view from the top of the steps that lead up to the fort is worth the climb from the small dinghy dock. Some of the fort's cannons faced the mainland as they were used by the eighteenth century English colonists to beat off attacks by the French and the Black Caribs.

Kingstown is readily accessible by bus or taxi, and a visit by either to the wild, unspoilt interior of Saint Vincent is a must. The Botanical Gardens and Fort Charlotte, just outside Kingstown, should not be missed. The Botanical Gardens are of particular interest as they have a direct descendant of a breadfruit tree that was carried to Saint Vincent by Captain Bligh of *Bounty* fame. He sailed to Saint Vincent from Tahiti on his next ship after the *Bounty*, the *Providence*, with a cargo of 500 Polynesian breadfruit saplings. Soon breadfruit trees were growing throughout the Caribbean and their fruit quickly became the staple diet of the plantation slaves.

Montreal Gardens, in nearby Mesopotamia Valley, are less well kept than the Botanical Gardens but they are a pleasant bus ride away from Kingstown or Young Island Cut. And if you have a free day do not forget the north of the island - perhaps a hike to the top of the volcano Soufrière if the sky is clear, or a visit by car and motor boat to the waterfall at Grand Baleine.

Customs and Immigration
A new post is planned at the Cut, but until then you have to enter and clear at Kingstown or Bequia.

Blue Lagoon

This is a well sheltered lagoon, but unfortunately often crowded with local yachts and charter yachts from CSY and Bimini Yachting Vacations. Beware of the reefs that extend from east of Young Island.

Approach
There are two possible entrances. The one in the north west is the easier and is well marked by stakes. Depending on the state of the tide the depth of the channel varies from 1.8 to just over 2 metres. The southern passage is deeper, about 3 metres, but is unmarked and thus more dangerous, so enter only in calm conditions.

Anchorage

Keep away from the CSY mooring chains in the middle of the lagoon and anchor in depths of water that vary from 4 to 10 metres in good holding black mud.

Ashore

You can leave the dinghy on the beach by CSY. Both charter companies will give help if you have engine problems and it is sometimes possible to take on fuel and water at their docks. The charter companies have good restaurants and they will allow you to use their telephones. In Calliaqua there is a fibreglass boat builder (Buhler) who carries out repair work. There are supermarkets near the airport and of course Kingstown is only a bus ride away.

Charts

British Admiralty: 791 General, 501 Details
USA: 25484 General
Imray Iolaire: B30 General (and Mustique) and details

Radio Station, Frequency and Times of Weather Bulletin

Radio St Vincent: 705 kHz

Airport

Inter-island airport at Joshua near Kingstown. Tel: 4011

THE GRENADINE ISLANDS

Only a short sail from Saint Vincent, the Grenadine Islands stretch along a south south west line approximately 60 miles long that runs from Bequia in the north to Isle Ronde in the south. In and among the dozens of bays, coral reefs, islets and islands of the Grenadines are some of the most spectacular anchorages in the Caribbean - some say the world.

Like so many Caribbean islands the history of the Grenadines is tied up with the Caribs and the colonial struggles of Britain and France. Whosoever controlled Saint Vincent and Grenada controlled the Grenadines. The Grenadines finally became British in 1783 and remained British colonies until Saint Vincent and Grenada became independent. Today Saint Vincent administers all but two of the inhabited islands. These two, Carriacou and Petite Martinique, are in the south and are looked after by Grenada.

The northern Grenadines have embraced tourism and over the last few years some of the islands have been developed at an incredible pace. There are now sophisticated resorts where charter and cruising yachts are welcome at Palm Island, Petit Saint Vincent, Bequia and Union Island. In contrast Grenada's charming Carriacou and Petite Martinique have remained almost unchanged for over a quarter of a century.

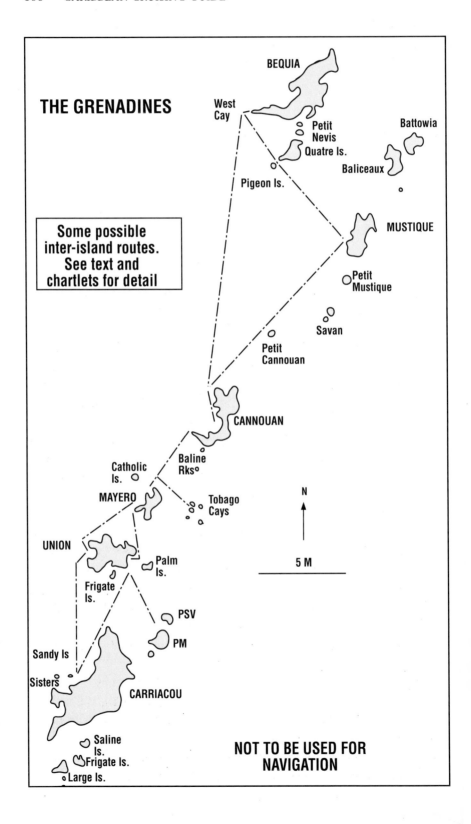

THE GRENADINES

BEQUIA

West Cay

Petit Nevis

Quatre Is.

Battowia

Baliceaux

Pigeon Is.

Some possible inter-island routes. See text and chartlets for detail

MUSTIQUE

Petit Mustique

Savan

Petit Cannouan

CANNOUAN

Baline Rks

Catholic Is.

MAYERO

Tobago Cays

UNION

Palm Is.

Frigate Is.

PSV

PM

Sandy Is

Sisters

CARRIACOU

N

5 M

Saline Is.

Frigate Is.

Large Is.

NOT TO BE USED FOR NAVIGATION

BEQUIA

Bequia has long been a Caribbean yachting centre, partly because the only way to the island is by boat, although an airport is planned and should be built by 1992. Bequians are descendants of Scottish farmers, American whalers, African slaves and French contrabandists, and the men are as strong and powerful as their genes are mixed. I will always be grateful to huge Augustus Olliverre who, when he should have been looking after his own boat, helped me pull my yacht off the beach when the eye of Hurricane Emily swept through the channel between Saint Vincent and Bequia. Bequians have the sea in their blood and a long tradition of boat building and trade. Islanders continue to leave Bequia to crew cargo ships and travel the world. Those who stay fish the cays and rocks off Bequia's coasts in tiny open boats.

Bequia used to be an important whaling station, and in the season (February to April) Bequians still hunt humpback and sperm whales from open boats, and tow the carcasses back to the whale station on the small offshore island of Petit Nevis. Wooden Bequia schooners continue to be built on the beach by eye and without plans. Today a 21 year old, two-masted wooden schooner, *Friendship Rose* works out of Admiralty Bay, making a daily trip across the Bequia Channel to Kingstown.

One of the largest wooden schooners built in the Lesser Antilles this century was the 165 ft long 178 ton *Gloria Colita*, which was constructed on the beach in Admiralty Bay. *Gloria Colita* was launched with much ceremony in 1939. Two years later she was found abandoned and awash in the Gulf Stream with her sails still set on the foremast and there was no sign of any storm damage. There was also no sign of the Spanish crew or her skipper Reg Mitchell, father of Saint Vincent's present Prime Minister J F 'Son' Mitchell.

Admiralty Bay

The town of Port Elizabeth is situated at the head of Admiralty Bay and the anchorages are off the town.

Approach
This is best by day and is without difficulty. The trip south *from Saint Vincent* to Admiralty Bay is usually an easy reach, but the westerly currents can be strong. When the trade winds blow against an easterly tide the sea becomes steep and confused - especially off Bequia's north east coast. The entrance to Admiralty Bay is situated about half way along the north west coast of Bequia and opens up as you approach. Pass the headland to port, giving Devil's Table shoal and Wash Rock, which is supposedly marked by a buoy, a wide berth. Head up the bay towards Port Elizabeth.

When *sailing north* from the island of Cannouan to West Cay, on the western tip of Bequia, you will probably be fairly hard on the wind - make allowance for the one to two knot westerly current you will experience during the 16 mile trip. Round West Cay and head up the bay and you will pass Moon Hole, a ruined house that looks as if it has been hollowed out of the cliff face, and nearby is a fantastic collection of houses carved out of the rock with open windows. These houses make up an exclusive resort for those wishing to take a special 'back to nature' vacation.

Do not enter Admiralty Bay at night. There ought to be a light on West Cay (Fl 10s 8M) and a sectored light behind the ferry dock in Port Elizabeth (Fl 4s WRG), with the white sector being the safe sector. Devil's Table buoy should flash red (Fl R 10s) as should a buoy in the middle of the bay (Fl R 4s). However the light on West Cay went out in 1989; the light on the dock is often obscured by the two ferries and the masts of the local schooners and rarely works; Devil's Table buoy is unlit and, at the time of going to press, there is no sign of the buoy in the middle of the bay.

Anchorage
There are four possibilities, with the most popular anchorages being

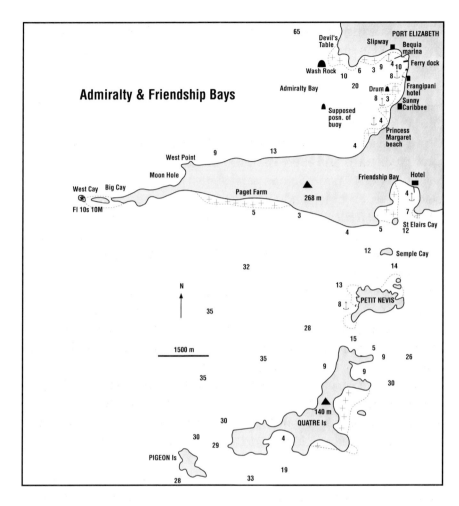

Admiralty & Friendship Bays

on the southern side of the bay. Coming from the north as you round Devil's Table shoal, golden-sanded Princess Margaret (or Tony Gibbons) beach is in front of you on the opposite side of the bay. Drop the anchor in depths of 4 to 5 metres in good holding sand. In the winter months a swell can make this anchorage uncomfortable.

Just north of Princess Margaret beach there is an anchorage off the Sunny Caribee Plantation House, but watch out for the shoals that come out from the shore as you approach from the south. There is also a shallow water reef that extends some way offshore south of the Frangipani hotel. The reef is sometimes marked by a rusty oil drum.

Most cruising yachts anchor off the Frangipani hotel, but although there is a convenient dinghy dock in front of the hotel the holding is poor in sandy clay, and the water is deep, 5 to 10 metres. When you leave your dinghy at the dock lock up the oars and outboard as there have been some thefts. It is possible to anchor at the head of Admiralty Bay, south of the ferry dock and opposite the church, but it is very deep close to the shore and the shelf is narrow.

The fourth anchorage is on the north side of the bay, to the west of the Bequia Marina fuel dock. The holding is quite good in sandy clay, and although the water is deep, between 6 and 10 metres, it is less crowded than the other anchorages. You are about ten minutes walk away from town and there is a good dinghy dock under the Harpoon Saloon. The Harpoon Saloon serves great meals and is a wonderful place for an evening sundowner. Be sure to anchor clear of the ferry dock as both ferries make daily trips to Kingstown (see below).

Ashore
The Frangipani hotel runs Frangipani Yacht Services where it is possible to make international telephone calls, to receive mail and send and receive cables. The poste restante address is: Yacht <>, Poste Restante, Frangipani Yacht Services, Box 1, Bequia, Saint Vincent, West Indies. You can go alongside the Bequia Marina fuel dock in the north of the bay and obtain diesel, fresh water and ice. The dock was damaged by a hurricane and a naval patrol boat, but there is enough of it left to be able to go alongside for an overnight stop.

Bequia Slipway is situated on the north side of the bay. The yard has a 100-ton railway haul and the management allow you to work on your boat. Bequia Slipway has showers, a laundry, a mechanical workshop and employs first class shipwrights to build or repair boats.

In Port Elizabeth there are two excellent chandleries (Bosun's Locker and Grenadines Yacht Equipment), a sailmaker (Lincoln Simmons sail loft), a superb fishing tackle shop west of the Bequia Slipway, a petrol station, a couple of bakers, a post office, a tourist office, a model boat shop, two banks, supermarkets, vegetable shops, boutiques, a bookshop selling charts and flags and a variety of waterside restaurants from Pizzerias to top quality hotels serving West Indian and French cuisine. Scuba diving can be arranged from the Sunny Caribbee, or the Clubhouse next to the Frangipani Hotel.

There are interesting walks from Port Elizabeth to Friendship Bay, and the settlements at Hope, Mount Pleasant, Spring or Industry, and at the end of the walk there is usually a beach, a restaurant or a bar, sometimes all three. If you arrive in Bequia around Christmas or at Easter (which is the time of the four- day Bequia Regatta) expect many yachts and a party atmosphere.

It is definitely worth taking a ferry to visit Kingstown and/or Saint Vincent - especially enjoyable is the early morning trip on the schooner *Friendship Rose*. She leaves at 0630 every morning and returns from Kingstown at 1230. The motor ferry makes two trips a day, departing at 0630 (after the schooner) and returning at 1000, and again departing from Port Elizabeth at 1440 and returning at 1630.

Customs and Immigration
Yachts can enter and clear Saint Vincent and its dependent Grenadine Islands at Port Elizabeth and this is much easier than entering and clearing at Kingstown on Saint Vincent. In Port Elizabeth the customs and immigration building is situated near the ferry dock.

I would advise you to enter and clear all the Saint Vincent administrated Grenadines at either Bequia (enter here when sailing south) or Union Island (enter here when sailing north). From both islands you can obtain permission to visit all of Saint Vincent's dependencies which include Cannouan, and the Tobago Cays.

The office hours for customs and immigration in both islands is the same: Monday to Friday, 0900 to 1200, and 1300 to 1600; Saturdays 0900 to 1200. Overtime is charged from 1600 to1800 during weekdays and 1200 to 1600 on Saturdays. Overtime is also charged on Sundays and Public Holidays from 0900 to1200 and 1500 to1800.

Friendship Bay

An unfrequented anchorage on the south side of Bequia; the beach is magnificent, the water clear and the bathing superb. The Friendship Bay Resort offers first class cuisine, a beach bar and a party every Saturday night.

Approach
From the north give West Cay a clear berth and motor sail along the south side of the island with the wind usually dead ahead. *From the south* pass either side of Petit Nevis, but there are reefs extending to the south west of Petit Nevis and west of Semple Cay. When entering Friendship Bay keep to the middle of the headlands as reefs extend from St Elairs Cay to the mainland and off the eastern headland. Anchor west of the dock or tucked up in the north east corner of the bay. A swell can enter so a stern anchor is useful to stop you rolling.

Ashore

Water is available at the Friendship Bay Resort dock. If you decide to go alongside for water have a good look at the approach in your dinghy before you come stern or bow to as the bay is shallow and there is the occasional rock near the shore. There is scuba diving from the Resort and from nearby Bequia Beach Club. At the west end of the bay some basic stores can be obtained from a bar. I recommend a walk over to the fishing village west of the anchorage.

There is a daytime anchorage off **Petit Nevis** which is an inhabited island less than a mile away from Friendship Bay. The anchorage is in front of the dock in the south of the island which serves the whalers, and ashore there are interesting whaling artifacts. There is also a possible daytime anchorage in 3 to 4 metres about half way along, and under the lee of **Quatre Island**. The uninhabited islands of Baliceaux and Battowia do not offer any real anchorages as the currents are strong and they are open to the northerly swell. In calm conditions local fishermen sometimes use the difficult Landing Bay anchorage in the south of the Baliceaux Island. The north end of Battowia is lit (Gp Fl (2) 20s 708ft 8M).

The fishing is exceptionally good all around these islands but the government of Saint Vincent and the Grenadines is taking an increasingly firm attitude in its attempt to protect the marine environment. A recent government regulation bans all visitors from spear fishing anywhere in the Grenadines, although visitors are allowed to line fish for their own consumption outside specially protected areas where all forms of fishing by both locals and visitors are banned. The protected areas around Bequia are Devil's Table and Quatre Island. Lobsters, once numerous, are becoming increasingly rare and the government has now made it illegal to buy lobsters in the closed/breeding season, which runs from1 May to 30 September. It is also illegal to buy a 'berried' female (a lobster with eggs under its tail) and all lobsters must be over nine inches in length before they are caught. Failure to comply with any of these fishing regulations could bring a $5 000 fine!

Charts

British Admiralty: 25482 Grenadines general, 501 Detail Admiralty Bay
USA: 25483 General
Imray Iolaire: B30 St Vincent and details, B31Bequia to Carriacou

MUSTIQUE

Mustique is the most easterly of the inhabited Grenadine Islands and is the second (or third) home of some of the super rich and famous - Princess Margaret, Raquel Welch, Mick Jagger and David Bowie all have houses on this exclusive, private island. It is a fun place to visit, the houses are interesting, there is a spectacular wreck and deep bays for snorkelling and scuba diving, and golden-sanded beaches for bathing. Mustique's only anchorage is on the west, leeward side of the island in Grand (or Britannia) Bay.

Grand Bay

Approach

From any direction the current is strong and westerly. The most popular approach to Mustique is *from Admiralty Bay*, Bequia. Yachts pass West Cay to port and beat towards Quatre Island to pass between it and Pigeon Island. The other obvious routes from Bequia are through the passages between Petit Nevis and Quatre Island, or Semple Cay and Petit Nevis, but these routes are generally avoided as, within the passages, the current can be very strong and the seas rough. Friendship Bay in the south of Bequia makes a good departure point. The northerly trip from Cannouan to Mustique is rarely attempted in the winter months as the winds are from the north east and the island is almost dead upwind.

Yachts sometimes sail to Mustique *from Saint Vincent*, a fast easy trip in the winter months. If you come that way give the north end of Bequia a good clearance as rough seas and the strong westerly

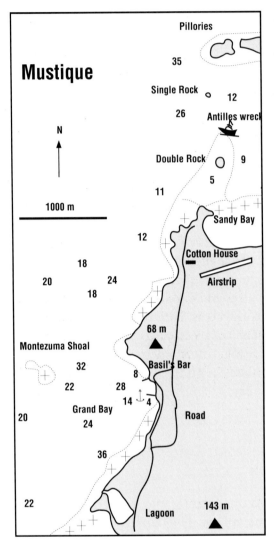

currents can set you down on to the island, which is a lee shore. Sailing over to Mustique from Saint Vincent or Friendship Bay you can see the wreck of the *Antilles*, put on the reef in 1971 as her captain tried to give his passengers a closer look at Mustique.

As you approach, head for either the north or the south of Grand Bay as there is a dangerous, usually unmarked, reef, Montezuma Shoal, in the middle of the bay and about 650 metres from the beach. Also look out for the shoals that extend some distance offshore in the south part of Grand Bay.

Anchorage

Anchor close to the jetty in Grand Bay in a depth of about 4 metres in good holding sand. There is almost always an unpleasant swell that creeps into the bay so a stern anchor to keep bow on to the waves is generally a must to prevent rolling.

Ashore

Basil's Bar is on a small pier in the Bay. It serves excellent food and has open air 'jump ups' to live bands on Wednesday and Saturday nights. A small shop selling basics is situated opposite the pier and there is a similar shop in the village at the top of the hill that overlooks the Bay. The island can be easily explored on foot, but it is possible to hire motor bikes, taxis or even horses. A superbly restored, eighteenth century hotel/restaurant, the Cotton House, is situated by the island's airstrip. At the hotel bar by the fresh water pool you have a wonderful view over the wreck of the *Antilles*. The Cotton House has a boutique and a dive shop, and if you make a reservation for dinner (VHF ch 68) they will pick you up.

If you take the dinghy to dive off the *Antilles* be careful, as in the vicinity of the wreck the currents are very strong. No less dangerous are the numerous sand sharks that bask in the bottom of the next bay south of Grand Bay. They are supposed to be harmless, but do not annoy them as one scuba diver I know did to his cost. Remember that visitors to any of the Grenadines are not allowed to spear fish; the protected areas in Mustique, where every form of fishing is banned, are Grand Bay and Sandy Bay.

A daytime anchorage exists off to the north west of Savan Island but do not anchor too close to the shore as there are steep breakers and dangerous shoals. The next island with a classical anchorage lies about 11 miles south west of Mustique and is quiet, unspoilt Cannouan.

Customs and Immigration
Mustique is a private island.

Charts
British Admiralty: 2872 General
French: 3206 General
USA: 25482 General and Cannouan detail
Imray Iolaire: B31 Bequia to Carriacou

Airport
Inter-island airstrip, near Cotton Hotel.

CANNOUAN ISLAND

Cannouan (pronounced 'canawan' and sometimes written as Canouan) is administered from Saint Vincent. It was once an important nineteenth century whaling station and then much of Cannouan was privately owned. There were also some large estates, and the remains of the cotton plantations, the estate houses and the estate owners' church can be seen in the north east of the island. A hurricane destroyed its roof in 1921 and soon after the estates were purchased by the crown which divided up the land and sold it to the local inhabitants. Today the 700 inhabitants of the island are relatively poor, there are few roads and most of the houses are still lit with paraffin lamps. Cannouan has some spectacular walks and is one of the most peaceful and lonely of all the Caribbean islands described in this guide. The east coast of the island is a protected area where any form of fishing is prohibited.

Charlestown Bay

Cannouan's main town is Charlestown, situated in Charlestown Bay located in the middle of the island's west coast.

Approach
This is an easy approach by day. Sailing *south from the western tip of Bequia* you should have a nice reach to Cannouan's main anchorage in Charlestown Bay. As you approach, Glass Hill in the south west corner of the island stands out as a separate island, but the isthmus joining it to the rest of Cannouan soon becomes apparent. Nearer

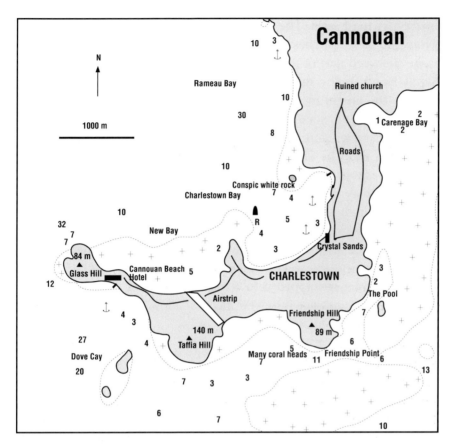

Cannouan, Petit Cannouan Island, which is supposed to be lit (Gp Fl(4) 40s 252ft 8M), will help you fix your position.

From Mustique you will sail more or less down wind to Cannouan. Steer to be west of, but close to, Petit Cannouan Island. Three knot westerly going currents can occur off Petit Cannouan, and the sea can be lumpy and rough off the north coast of Cannouan.

When coming *from the north* travel down the west coast of the island and look for a white (bird limed) rock in the north end of the bay and a red buoy in the middle. Head for the red buoy - there is a passage on either side but close to the buoy. There are leading lights marked on the charts but none were functioning at the time of going to press, nor are they easily visible from the sea. When coming from the south pass Glass Hill and round up into the bay.

Anchorage
Anchor near the brokendown dock in the north of the bay and to the east of the white rock. The holding is not good in a depth of about 5

metres on hard sand. The green coloured water makes it difficult to avoid the weed patches but if you can dig in the anchor this is the more sheltered part of the bay. The other anchorage is off the Crystal Sands Hotel in the middle of the bay (where the holding is better than in the north) in depths of 3 to 5 metres in clearer water, looser sand and fewer weed patches - but the swell is worse. Breakers sometimes make landing difficult in front of the Crystal Sands Hotel but if you take the dinghy to the north of the bay you can usually scramble ashore without getting wet.

On the way in to the anchorage from the north you will pass secluded anchorages in Anse Guyac (just enough room for one yacht) and also in Rameau Bay. In the south west of the island there are supposed to be anchorages in New Bay; just north of the airstrip, and the other behind the reef at the west end of New Bay - which at one time was to be developed into a marina. Nothing has come of the marina and the passage into New Bay is shallow and difficult: the area is best left alone.

Ashore

Inter-island steamers regularly visit Charlestown Bay and, with much commotion, passengers and stores are ferried to and from the beach near the Crystal Sands Hotel. This hotel has a bar and serves ordinary meals. A wonderful little rum shop nearby sells paraffin and locally produced and very powerful 'Jack Iron' rum by the coke bottle. There are superb walks north from the Crystal Sands Hotel that eventually lead to the ruined church and cotton estates. If you take the north easterly track up the hill from Charlestown village, past the school and church, you will have scenic views of the windward side of the island that are some of the best in the Caribbean. In the town there is a post office and a shop selling a few basics and you will be offered fish, lobsters and conch (lambis) by the local fishermen. Make sure you buy lobsters only in season, which runs from 1 October to 31 April; that way you avoid a large fine and help maintain lobster stocks.

Cannouan Beach Hotel

For a good long walk take money, swimming gear and a towel and head for the airstrip in the south west of the island. Shortly after the air strip, and almost on the windward side of the island, you will unexpectedly come upon a very sophisticated French resort, the Cannouan Beach Hotel. An excellent restaurant, a bar, a dive shop and a superb beach complete with crashing Atlantic rollers and golden sands are all to hand. The only drawback is that fresh water tends to be in short supply as it brought in by barge from Saint Vincent. Under settled conditions there is an anchorage off the hotel by the jetty and behind Dove Cay but, because of the swell, it can be very uncomfortable and it is best thought of as a daytime stop. Some brave sailors take their boats into the bay behind Friendship Point and continue round into an anchorage known locally as **The Pool** - this is definitely not a classical Caribbean anchorage.

South of Cannouan Island is Mayero Island, and not far from there are the Tobago Cays - the most famous anchorage in the Antilles.

Customs and Immigration
Cannouan is a Saint Vincent dependency. Obtain permission to visit Cannouan from either Bequia or Union Island.

Charts
British Admiralty: 2872 General
French: 3206 General
USA: 25482 General and Cannouan detail
Imray Iolaire: B31 Bequia to Carriacou, B32 Cannouan to Carriacou

Airport
Inter-island airstrip near Cannouan Beach Hotel.

MAYERO ISLAND

Mayero (sometimes Mayreau) Island is privately owned by a Saint Vincent family. It was once the property of a French colonial family who, fleeing the British at the end of the eighteenth century, immigrated there from Carriacou. Because of this French influence the tiny population of Mayero, unlike the rest of the Grenadines, is mainly Roman Catholic. Until recently a French Dominican priest, Father Dionne, lived and worked on the island, and during his 20 years' stay he and the islanders not only built the church that stands on the side of the hill at the head of Saline Bay but also a substantial communal rain water cistern. Father Dionne was a powerful man: he was the island's religious leader and he also controlled the island's water, carrying with him wherever he went the key to the cistern. Today Father Dionne has retired and most of the islanders now have their own cisterns.

Mayero, once very poor, is now relatively busy and prosperous thanks to the recent tourist development near Salt Whistle Bay, the island's proximity to popular Tobago Cays and the frequent visits made to the island by passenger ships. In season the island's two main anchorages, Salt Whistle Bay in the north west of the island, and larger Saline Bay in the south west, are often crowded with charter yachts. At increasingly regular intervals Saline Bay becomes saturated with tourists, put ashore from the cruise ships that visit the Grenadine Islands in ever increasing numbers. The islanders sell souvenirs and fish to their many clients.

The fishing and snorkelling is everywhere excellent around the island but note that the whole of Mayero's coast is a protected area and fishing in any form is banned.

Salt Whistle Bay

Approach

From Cannouan and the north sail down to the west side of Cannouan to Glass Hill - or Glossy Hill as it is sometimes known. When you round Glass Hill there will be a confusing mass of islands in front of you. Way over on your port bow will be the fabulous Tobago Cays (and you can sail there direct from Cannouan, see pages 126-7) but the Tobago Cays are best visited from Mayero.

Mayero Island lies in front of Union Island. Union is identified by the sharply peaked, 226 metre high, Pinnacle. West of the Pinnacle the land drops away and then rises again towards the four other peaks on Union - creating a well defined U-shape in Union's distant outline. Just to the east of the Pinnacle, and some four miles north of

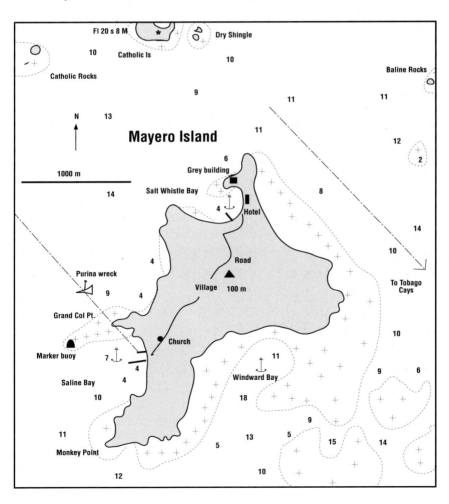

Union Island, is Catholic Island, another good landmark that lies about a mile north west of Mayero. To arrive at Salt Whistle Bay set a course to allow for a possible two knot westerly current and continuously check your position by taking bearings of the 'Pinnacle U', Channel Rocks, Baline Rocks and Catholic Island. There is an unreliable light on Catholic Island (Fl 20s 144 ft 8M) and at the time of going to press there are no buoys off the north of Mayero Island. Give Dry Shingle rocks that lie to the east of Catholic Island a wide berth, and identify an empty grey cement building on the northern headland of Salt Whistle Bay. Keep to the centre of the entrance to the bay.

From the south pass along the west, leeward coast of Mayero taking great care to avoid the reef that extends about half a mile off shore to the south west off Grand Col Point. After this reef the north west coast of Mayero can be closed, and the southern headland rounded to enter Salt Whistle Bay. Look out for the grey building on the northern headland to help identify the entrance to the Bay. The anchorage will only take about 12 yachts.

Anchorage
Anchor anywhere inside the bay; the further in, the less the swell enters. The depth varies from 3 to 6 metres and the bottom is sand, which is sometimes hard to penetrate - especially with a CQR anchor.

Ashore
In season the tourist development amongst the palm trees offers a bar and a restaurant, but take mosquito repellent if you are ashore around dusk. A pleasant walk with good views is by the path that leads up the hill to the village, and another interesting one is the windward beach on the east side of the tourist development.

Saline Bay

The main and largest anchorage on Mayero is Saline Bay.

Approach
From the north or west be sure to give the reef that stretches west and south west of Grand Col Point a good clearance as you approach the anchorage. The 'buoy' (a rusty oil drum) that marks it at present should be given a wide berth as it is moored right on the reef. The

A quiet anchorage in the Grenadines

wreck on the north side of the reef is the *HMS Purin*, a World War I steam gunship that clipped the reef and sank one night as she was setting out on patrol. *From the south* there are no difficulties.

Anchorage

Anchor in front of the jetties in good holding sand in depths of 3 to 4 metres. There is sometimes a swell, so a second anchor to keep you head on to the waves is advisable.

Ashore

In season, the beach is crowded a couple of days each week with passengers and boats from the cruise ships that visit the island. The locals do a brisk business from their permanently erected souvenir stalls which can be seen some way out from the shore.

Dennis' Hideaway bar/restaurant is a good place to stop for refreshments when climbing the road that leads away from the bay, past the church and up to the village at the top of the hill where the views of the Tobago Cays and Union Island are breathtaking. If you continue along this path you will after a very enjoyable walk eventually come to Salt Whistle Bay.

When in Salt Whistle or Saline Bays if you call 'Scuba Safaris' on VHF ch 16 or 68 they will pick you up from your boat for a dive over the gunship wreck which lies some 6 metres below the surface. If you just want to snorkel over the Grand Col Point reef and the wreck take care for there are strong currents. The wreck lies on a transit that runs from the middle of the northerly jetty in Saline Bay and Grand Col Point.

Windward Bay

There is an anchorage under good weather conditions on the windward side of Mayero in Windward Bay. Round Monkey Point and navigate the yacht by eye between the reefs that lie just offshore and about a quarter of a mile offshore. Anchor in depths of around 10 metres, but this anchorage is strictly for the adventurous.

Customs and Immigration
Mayero is a private island.

Charts
British Admiralty: 2872 General
French: 3206 General
USA: 25482 General and Cannouan detail
Imray Iolaire: B31 Bequia to Carriacou, B32 Cannouan to Carriacou.

THE TOBAGO CAYS

The reefs off the Tobago Cays offer some of the best underwater scenery in the Caribbean. Horseshoe Reef, which guards the Cays, is bathed in a warm clear sea brim full of brightly coloured fish and fantastically shaped coral. A visit to the Cays is a must, if only for the snorkelling. The voyage is not too difficult, even for the relatively inexperienced sailor, providing you sail to the Cays from Mayero Island - and keep on the transits!

Snorkelling over the reef, if the Orinoco current is not too full of green algae to obscure visibility, you will see the coral drop away tens of metres to the sea bed. Sharks live in the deep gloom on the other side of the reef, but because of the abundance of food they almost never attack and rarely come over to the shallow side (although a few years ago a huge one, looking very hungry, swept past me while I was swimming on the shallow side). The Tobago Cays' anchorage in the sands behind Horseshoe Reef is open to the full force of the trade winds but you are normally well protected from the sea by the surrounding Horseshoe and not too distant World's End Reefs. You are quite safe providing the weather is fine (which it is usually) and the anchor is well dug in. At night the trade winds whistle eerily through the rigging and you have the incredible impression of being at anchor in the middle of an ocean (especially in the wet season when the dark high clouds of the squalls come sweeping in).

There are a few buoys and one or two lights near the Tobago Cays but they are all extremely unreliable so *never* sail at night. The Tobago Cays are a national park and in order to conserve the marine environment any form of fishing in the area by locals or visitors is forbidden.

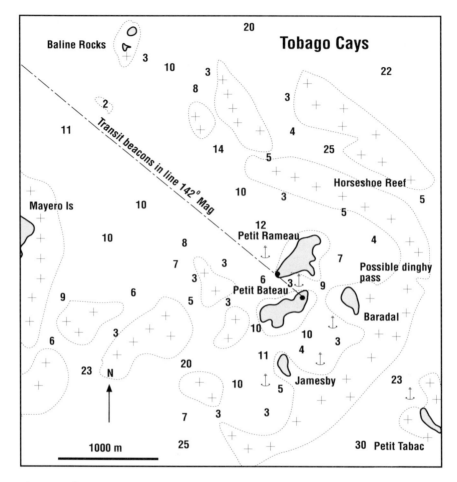

Approach

The best approach *from any direction* is from the leeward side of Mayero Island. Ideally anchor for the night at either Salt Whistle or Saline Bays and in the morning approach the Cays from the north west coast of Mayero. Round the north of Mayero Island and either make a beat of many short tacks, or a motor sail, up to Tobago Cays, keeping your course as best you can on the black and white transit beacons that line up on 142° Magnetic.

However, if you do decide to day sail *directly from Cannouan* to the Tobago Cays without a stop at Mayero (and I do not advise this) pass well to leeward, west of Baline Rocks, and be sure to watch out for the shoal that lies about half a mile south west of the Rocks. You will be sailing along a course that leads about half way between Mayero Island and the Baline Rocks, and by keeping south of a bearing of 128° Magnetic on the north end of Petit Rameau you will clear this shoal. Head for the gap between Petit Rameau and Petit Bateau and come on to the two black and white transit beacons that line up on 142° Magnetic for a safe transit into the Cays. It is also possible to pass to the east, the windward side, of the Baline Rocks. Sail between them and the end of Horseshoe Reef that lies south east of the Baline Rocks. Sail through the gap until you pick up the transit on the beacons.

Jamesby and Baradal Islands

Anchorage

In season often the only place left at the Cays is on the windward side of Baradal or Jamesby Islands. Anchor as close to the Horseshoe Reef as you see fit - the holding is good in loose sand and in depths of around 3 to 5 metres. There is another anchorage under the lee of Jamesby Island. It is also possible to anchor in 3 to 5 metres of water in the channel between Petit Rameau and Petit Bateau, but here the holding is poor and you will probably need to use a bow and a stern anchor as there are strong currents flowing back and forth through the cut. Large yachts sometimes anchor in the lee of Petit Rameau in depths of around 10 metres.

Ashore

There are some beautiful sandy beaches on the islands and they gradually shelve for easy bathing. Local fishermen will offer you fish and coral and turtle shell jewellery. You may also be offered lobsters and turtle shells. Please remeber to buy lobsters only in the correct season, and you should note that recent government regulations now forbid the fishermen to sell the shells from turtles that weigh less than 85 lbs.

To leave the Tobago Cays the safest way out is the way you came in. There are southern passages, and the best is to the south of Jamesby Island and north of Sand Cay, but I would not recommend any of them. For the brave and experienced there are also daytime anchorages behind Petit Tabac and south east of Egg Reef behind World's End Reef.

Customs and Immigration

Before visiting the Tobago Cays yachts should have entered St Vincent and its Grenadine dependencies at either Bequia or Union Islands.

Charts
British Admiralty: 2872 General
French: 3206 General
USA: 25482 General and Cannouan detail
Imray Iolaire: B31 Bequia to Carriacou, B32 Cannouan to Carriacou.

The anchorage at Petit Saint Vincent, The Grenadines

UNION ISLAND

During the late nineteenth century after the slaves were freed and the sugar cane markets disappeared Union Island's prosperity and population, like most other Caribbean islands, declined. In the twentieth century tourism has for many Caribbean islands been their economic salvation, and the Grenadines are no exception. During the last 20 years, and because of the proximity of the Tobago Cays, Union Island has become an important yachting centre in the Grenadines. Nowadays, close to the island's capital, Clifton, there is an airstrip, a sophisticated French resort - the Anchorage Yacht Club - and a slipway for yachts. Much of the island's economy depends on the many charter and cruising yachts who work from, or visit, the island.

Union Island's population of some 1 600 resides in Clifton and Ashton. There is a good anchorage off Ashton village behind Frigate Island and another in Chatham Bay in the west of the island, but the best anchorage is in Clifton Harbour at the east end of the island.

Clifton Harbour

Clifton Harbour is one of the few harbours in the Caribbean that is on the windward side of an island. Clifton Harbour lies behind Thompson and Newlands Reefs and because of a reef inside the harbour, within these outer reefs, there are two entrances.

Approach
Do so by day only, as the buoys marking the reefs are not always correctly positioned and not always lit. *From the north* round Red

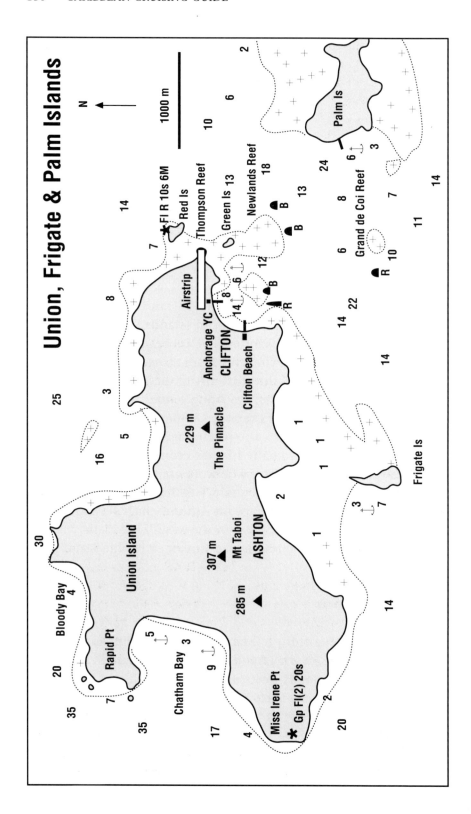

Union, Frigate & Palm Islands

N

1000 m

Island, which supposedly has a light (Fl R 10s 128ft 6M) and keep well to the east of Thompson Reef, Green Island and Newlands Reef which extends south west from Red Island. Leave the two black buoys (Fl 4s) off Newlands Reef to starboard, and as the position of all the buoys is uncertain, they need to be given a good clearance. The safest approach is to sail almost over to Palm Island before you turn west for the eastern entrance to Clifton Harbour. The most spectacular and breezy anchorages are behind Thompson and Newlands Reefs and up towards Green Island.

When approaching Clifton Harbour *from the south* it is important to keep clear of drying Grand de Coi Reef, which lies about half a mile west of Palm Island, and because of the swell is sometimes hard to see. The best passage is to the west of this dangerous reef, so leave the red buoy (which is supposed to be lit, Fl R 4s) that marks the west end of Grand de Coi, well to starboard.

The south west corner of the central reef within Clifton Harbour is marked by a concrete block - the remains of a light - and a black buoy (Fl 4s). When coming through the western entrance to the harbour leave the red buoy, which marks the end of a reef that extends from the shore, to port. The black buoy and concrete block are left to starboard.

Anchorage

East of the central reef and behind Thompson and Newlands Reefs, anchor in depths between 6 to 9 metres in good holding sand. Do not be tempted to pick up an empty mooring as there is a good chance that it belongs to a charter yacht on a visit to the Tobago Cays.

The other anchorages are to the west and north of the central reef. Some yachts anchor off the Clifton Beach Hotel while others prefer to anchor near the fuel dock, south of the Anchorage Yacht Club. The water is deep, 10 to 14 metres, on the west side of the central reef and around 8 metres off the Anchorage Yacht Club. In both places the holding is good, but you may find it difficult to break through the bottom weed, or to dig the anchor flukes into hard packed sand.

Ashore

Diesel, water and ice are available at the Anchorage Yacht Club fuel dock. Fresh water is distilled by the Club from salt water so it is expensive and sometimes rare. The Anchorage Yacht Club has a first class restaurant and bar, showers (when water is plentiful), telephones, a boutique, a laundry and a poste restante. There is a shark pool in front of the hotel, although most of the sharks are harmless nurse sharks.

Just to the east of the Anchorage Yacht Club is a slipway with two railway hauls that can accommodate yachts displacing up to six or 30 tons. There is no chandlery on the island and fresh water for cleaning is expensive. The yard is very picturesque and fine for a bottom scrub, but if you have any major work to do make sure you bring everything with you - or else you might have to fly to Martinique or Grenada for that important screw you forgot.

The Sunny Grenadines restaurant/bar on the west side of Clifton Harbour sells water, gas and petrol from their dock, but check with the owner and have a look at the dock before you come in. You can also buy paraffin by the bottle in Clifton village where there are plenty of food shops as well as a post office, a bank and a bakery.

Scuba diving can be arranged from the Anchorage Hotel and Scuba Safari just west of the hotel (VHF ch 68). The Clifton Beach Hotel serves meals as do a variety of other bars and restaurants. It is possible to walk/scramble to the top of The Pinnacle (229 metres) and the taller Mount Taboi (307 metres).

Customs and Immigration
Clifton Harbour is a port of entry (or departure) for Saint Vincent and the Grenadines. First go to the customs building that is situated just off the beach before you arrive at the Clifton Beach Hotel, and then over to immigration which is on the north side of the airstrip. All are within easy walking distance.

Frigate Island

This delightfully quiet anchorage is situated behind Frigate Island about three quarters of a mile off the village of Ashton. Note that a 1-metre shallow extends from Ashton village to the north of Frigate Island.

Approach
From the north, be sure to keep clear of Grand de Coi Reef and the coral reef that extends half a mile to the east of Frigate Island. *From the south and west*, keep some distance off Queensberry Point on Union Island.

Anchorage
Tuck yourself up behind Frigate Island and anchor in good holding sand in depths of between 2.5 and 3.5 metres.

Ashore
The village of Ashton is accessible by dinghy.

Chatham Bay

This is a delightfully secluded anchorage on the west side of Union Island. The bay is often full of leaping fish, and the pelicans are very active off Rapid Point. The wind sometimes comes screeching down into the bay from off the hills but it will do you no harm.

Approach
From the north, it is an easy sail from Mayero Island to Rapid Point. Do not pass too close to Rapid Point as there are some offlying rocks. *From the south* there are no dangers; round Miss Irene Point and enter the bay. Miss Irene Point light (Gp Fl (2) 20s 469 ft 8M) has not functioned for some time.

Anchorage
The best spot is up in the north east corner of the bay in depths of between 3 and 5 metres in good holding sand. Some skippers prefer to anchor in the south east corner of the bay as they are less disturbed by the seine net fishermen who will always ask you to move.

Ashore
Nothing.

About a mile south east of Union Island is Palm Island. Yachts often base themselves in Clifton Harbour and sail here for the day.

Palm Island

On Palm (or Prune) Island there is a famous 'get away from it all' resort of small bungalows hidden behind palm trees that was created largely through the efforts of John Caldwell who, some years ago, took out a 99-year lease on Prune Island from the Saint Vincent government. He renamed it Palm Island in commemoration of all the palm trees he had planted and he and his family set about converting a tiny mosquito-infested island into an internationally famous resort. John Caldwell was already well known before he came to Prune Island for his best-selling book, *Desperate Voyage* in which he hilariously, and also seriously, described his attempts to sail to Australia from Panama after the end of World War II. Palm Island anchorage would be ideal if it were not for the swell, as it is off one of the most beautiful beaches in the Grenadines.

Approach
From the north keep to the middle of the channel between Green Island and Palm Island before turning towards the beach on the leeward side of Palm Island. There is a reef that extends about a quarter of a mile north of Palm Island.

From the south the safest route is to pass to the west of Grand de Coi Reef and, leaving the red buoy on the starboard bow, head up towards Clifton Harbour before turning to the east and the Palm Island anchorage.

Anchorage
Anchor in a depth of 6 metres in fair holding sand off the jetty. The anchorage is nearly always uncomfortable because of the swell, so it is better to spend the day here and return to the calmer waters of Clifton Harbour for the night - but if you do not mind the roll there is no reason not to spend the night.

Ashore
Snorkel and swim off the island's wonderful golden-sanded beaches on both the windward and leeward coasts. There is a restaurant, a bar, a small shop and a boutique just off the beach and opposite the anchorage. Palm Island is a protected region and any form of fishing is prohibited on the surrounding reefs and beaches.

Charts
British Admiralty: 2872 General
French: 3206 General
USA: 25482 General
Imray Iolaire: B31 Bequia to Carriacou

PETIT SAINT VINCENT

About two and a half miles south of Prune or Palm Island is the most southern of the Saint Vincent dependencies - Petit Saint Vincent. PSV, as it is known locally, is like Prune Island in that it has recently been converted from a deserted island into an internationally famous resort. The anchorage is less affected by swell than that of Palm Island.

The anchorage in PSV is off the south west corner in a region that is strewn with reefs and coral heads - approach the island with caution. The island's reefs and beaches are a protected area and any form of fishing is forbidden.

Approach

From the north from Union Island it is possible to pass between two small sand islands, Pinese and Mopion, but take care as Pinese has a habit of disappearing beneath the waves! Mopion is a few feet above water and the island has a distinctive thatched shelter for daytime picnickers from the island resort. If you want to take the risk, navigate your way by eye through the two islands, steering about 163° Magnetic and heading for the highest point, 226 metres-high Piton, on Petite Martinique. The safer route is to sail west of Pinese and, taking bearings of PSV and Petite Martinique to fix your position, approach the PSV anchorage *from the west*.

Anchorage

In season the anchorage is often crowded. Anchor off the main dock in the south of the island or off the dinghy jetty below the hotel in depths of between 3 and 5 metres in good holding sand. Watch out for coral heads and a shallow reef about 400 metres offshore.

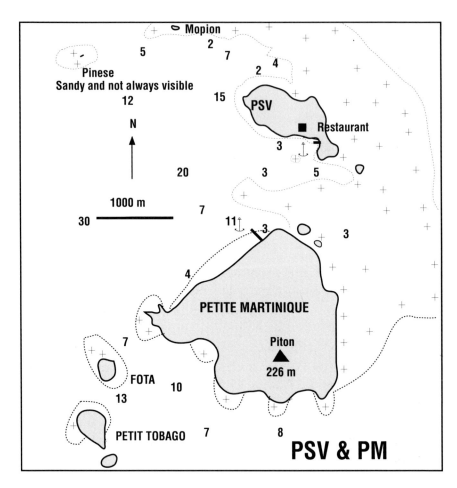

Ashore
The American-owned hotel offers a boutique, a bar and a restaurant with fantastic views over the anchorage. An early morning walk to the windward side of the island is a pleasant experience.
Customs and Immigration

Remember that Petit Saint Vincent is administered by Saint Vincent so yachts coming from the south should enter Saint Vincent and the Grenadines at Clifton Harbour before sailing over.

Charts
British Admiralty: 2872 General
French: 3206 General
USA: 25482 General
Imray Iolaire: B31 Bequia to Carriacou

PETITE MARTINIQUE

Less than a mile to the south of Petit Saint Vincent is the island of Petite Martinique, or PM as it is often called, and west of PM is the much larger island of Carriacou. Both PM and Carriacou are administered by the Grenadian government and both were relatively unaffected by the recent political upheavals that took place in Grenada. Tourism is non existent in PM and almost absent in Carriacou, even though Carriacou has an airstrip.

The 600 or so inhabitants of Petite Martinique, many of them of French origin, have, like the Bequians, long made a living from the sea in some form or another - whaling, fishing, crewing, boat building and smuggling.

Approach
No problems by day *from the north west or south west.* In the anchorage just off the jetty in the north west of the island there are always several moored inter-island trading schooners waiting to unload cargo or setting out for long voyages often as far north as Saint Barts.

Anchorage
The anchorage off PM is not a good one as a swell always manages to curl around the island. However, if you can stomach the rolling, a visit ashore is worthwhile as there are some long, interesting walks and the island has a large number of rum shops in which to recover.

Customs and Immigration
Since the island is looked after by Grenada and there are no resident custom officials, if you are sailing down from the north, in theory at

least, you have to enter at Hillsborough, the capital of Carriacou, before going ashore on PM.

Charts
British Admiralty: 2872 General
French: 3206 General
USA: 25482 General
Imray Iolaire: B31 Bequia to Carriacou

Ashore on Sandy Island off Carriacou. Union Island in the background

CARRIACOU

Carriacou's name comes from the Carib word 'Kayryouacou' meaning 'island surrounded by reefs'. As usual the Arawaks and then the Caribs were on the island long before the first recorded visit was made by a European - a French priest in 1656. The island was first settled by the French and, being efficient colonial administrators, in 1750 they conducted a census. It records that of the 199 people living on the island 92 were whites, 92 blacks and 15 mulattos (see *An Analysis of the 1750 Carriacou Census* by Frances Kay Brinkley, published locally). In 1763, the Treaty of Paris made Carriacou a British colony. A British census was carried out in 1776 which records in 26 years there had been an enormous increase in the number of slaves - 3 153 were owned by 86 Scottish, English and French plantation owners who produced sugar, rum, coffee, cocoa and their main crop, cotton. Six times more cotton - 772 763 lbs - was produced than sugar (Frances Kay). Today Carriacou is the most populated of the Grenadine islands, with some 6 000 inhabitants, and they live by fishing and farming. It is also the largest island in the Grenadines and one of the least touched by tourism.

Like Bequia and Petite Martinique there is a strong tradition of seafaring on Carriacou. Large wooden schooners continue to be built without plans on the beaches at Tyrrel (sometimes written 'Tyrell') and Windward Bays, and the launching ceremonies still last all day when the huge boats are dragged into the sea by hundreds of well wishers. The Carriacou islanders have a reputation of being warm and friendly and they make everyone feel especially welcome when they host one of the great sailing events in the Grenadines - the 'Carriacou Regatta'. The regatta takes place during the first weekend in August

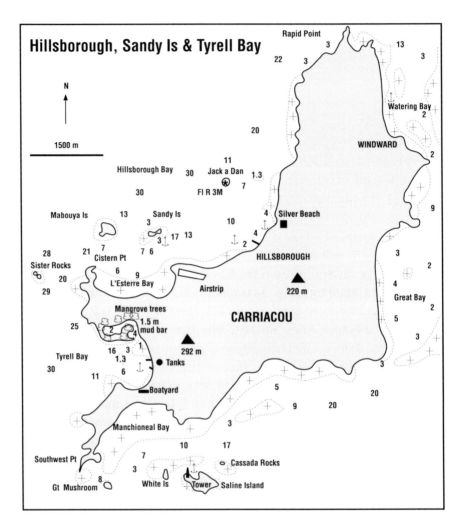

Hillsborough, Sandy Is & Tyrell Bay

and from all over the Grenadines working sail boats descend on Hillsborough, to race round Hillsborough Bay and the offshore islands. There are many class races and visiting cruising yachts are encouraged by the locals to enter the races and join in the fun.

Hillsborough Bay

Hillsborough, Carriacou's largest town, has about 600 inhabitants and its main street, which is lined with picturesque wooden houses, runs parallel with the beach. The dock is the focus of the town's activities and a crowd always gathers to meet or to say farewell to the inter-island schooners that run regular trips to Union Island and the north, and Grenada in the south. When coming from the north yachts have to enter Carriacou (and PM) at Hillsborough which is located in the middle of large Hillsborough Bay.

Approach

As for all the other Grenadine islands, only approach Carriacou by day. Coming *from the north*, sail down the island's west coast from Rapid Point. The safest route is to head about a mile offshore as you approach Jack a Dan rock as there is an unmarked shoal between the rock and the mainland. Leave Jack a Dan rock (supposedly lit, Fl R 3M) to port before turning for the new town dock.

Approaching Hillsborough *from the south* enter Hillsborough Bay between the Sister Rocks and Cistern Point on Carriacou. Pass either side of Mabouya and Sandy Islands and head towards the town dock. Mabouya was the name the Caribs called their evil gods, but you can pass fairly close to the island as it is steep to. However, L'Esterre Bay opposite Mabouya Island is shallow and rocky.

Anchorage

The traditional anchorage is off the jetty in depths of between 4 and 7 metres, but because the swell can make this spot uncomfortable, a better anchorage is to the north of the town dock and off the Silver Beach Hotel. Anchor in a depth of about 5 metres in good holding sand. The Silver Beach Hotel is planning a dinghy jetty and they have laid some buoys for visiting yachts.

Ashore

The Silver Beach Hotel has a restaurant and bar and they will organise scuba dives. In Hillsborough you will find a small vegetable market, a bank, a bakery, a post office, several shops selling basics and numerous local restaurants and rum shops. The museum is definitely worth a visit as are the rather run-down but charming Botanical Gardens not far from town.

Customs and Immigration

Customs is at the head of the town dock and immigration is just a short walk away. The hours are from 0800 to 1145 and 1400 to 1545 and overtime is payable outside these hours. If you enter Carriacou at Hillsborough and continue your journey south to Grenada you still have to report to the authorities in Grenada.

Sandy Island

Because of swell the anchorages off Hillsborough and the Silver Beach Hotel can be unpleasant, but a mile or two offshore is Sandy Island where, for some reason, the swell is often much reduced. On the southern side of Sandy Island there is a wonderful anchorage in golden sand and crystal clear water. The sea has almost broken Sandy Island into two separate islands so when you approach the island *from the south* head for this gap. Sandy Island is best approached *from the south west or south east* as there are shallow reefs to the north and west of the island.

Anchorage
The bottom comes up sharply from depths of around 17 metres to the anchorage where the depth is about 3 metres. The holding is good and because this is a lee shore the anchorage is considered by many to be only a daytime stop. But if the anchor is well set, and the weather settled, it is a delightful place in which to spend a night.

The snorkelling around Sandy Island is excellent but watch out for the strong currents off the most westerly islands. The area around Sandy Island is a national park and spear fishing is prohibited for locals and vsitors.

Carriacou's classical anchorage is in the south west of the island in vast Tyrrel or Great Carenage Bay.

Tyrrel Bay

Tyrrel (Tyrell) Bay is one of the largest, yet most peaceful, anchorages in the Grenadines. Off the bay in the north there is a mangrove lagoon that makes a possible hurricane hole. The brackish lagoon is worth exploring by dinghy as it is full of jumping fish, lumbering pelicans and clumps of mangrove oysters that grow on the roots of the trees. In season you will probably be offered the chance to sample the mangrove oysters by a local boatman, but they are not as good as salt water oysters.

Approach
From the north sail between Mabouya Island and Cistern Point and enter the bay. Head south of the centre of the bay because there is a

reef in the middle, with a least depth of 1.3 metres, which is sometimes marked by a buoy. When approaching *from the south*, keep south of the centre of the bay but also take care to avoid the shallows off the southern headland.

Anchorage

Drop the anchor north or south of the two jetties which run out from the shore in the middle of the bay and are situated near some conspicuous storage tanks. The water is around 4 metres deep and the bottom is hard sand and weed which is sometimes difficult to penetrate, especially in the south east corner of the bay.

Ashore

Carriacou Boat Builders are a growing concern in the south of Tyrrel Bay. The yard offers stainless steel and aluminium welding, aluminium dinghy construction, sail repairs and a woodwork shop. The yard is constructing a 100 ton railway haul. You can call Adventure Marine (VHF ch 16) for fibreglass, woodwork, sail repairs and outboard motor servicing and sales.

Two small supermarkets and restaurants are situated by the jetties in the middle of the bay and a small Italian restaurant, L'Aquilone, which has superb views, has been built on the top of the hill that rises behind the boatyard. Take a torch for the return journey if you decide to eat at L'Aquilone after dark (VHF ch 16 for a reservation) and leave your dinghy by the yard. A beach bar has recently been built in the south of the bay, and Cassada Bay Hotel (VHF ch 16), also with wonderful views, is a short taxi ride or a 25 minute walk away. Taxis also run to Hillsborough. If you are lucky you will see a schooner being built on the beach of Tyrrel Bay.

The mangrove lagoon off the north of Tyrrel Bay is the best hurricane shelter north of Grenada and south of Marigot Bay in Saint Lucia, but it is not ideal. There are two connected lagoons - in any suggestion of a hurricane the outer lagoon becomes very crowded, and the entrance to the inner lagoon has partially silted up. Moreover the entrance from Tyrrel Bay into the outer lagoon needs to be negotiated with care as it leads through a 1 metre shoal, so approach when the sun is high. Once safely through the shoal and into the outer lagoon there is a good depth of water, 4 to 5 metres, and the bottom is good holding sticky black mud. The larger inner lagoon is guarded by a 1.5 metre muddy bar and while it is usually possible to power your way through the soft mud you may have problems if your yacht's draught is any greater than 2 metres. Inside there is 2 to 4 metres of brackish, almost fresh, water but the inner lagoon is hot and airless and in hurricane force winds its western end, which is only very lightly protected by the mangrove trees, would be quite a flimsy barrier.

There are daytime anchorages behind **Frigate Island** and **Saline Island** off the south coast of Carriacou but these are best explored from Tyrrel Bay in settled conditions.

Watering Bay

There is an interesting anchorage off the town of Windward in the north east of Carriacou in Watering Bay. The entrance is from the north. Leave the sand bank to starboard before turning to starboard and anchoring among the fishing boats behind the sand bank in 2 metres. I have not been there but those who have say the entrance is relatively easy and the anchorage and the town interesting.

As you voyage further south away from Carriacou to Grenada you will see Diamond Rock or, as it is sometimes called, Kick 'em Jenny (perhaps, as Frances Kay suggests, deriving its unusual name from the French *Caye qui gene* - the Cay that disturbs). The island is steep to and there are no anchorages.

Still further south of Carriacou there is a possible anchorage in settled weather in the north west corner of **Ronde Isle** in Corn Store Bay in depths of about 5 metres but, as the holding is poor, use two anchors. Swell enters the bay and the current runs fast around the north and south headlands of the island. The passage between Ronde Isle and Grenada seems to be the meeting place of all manner of counter currents and the seas can be steep and irregular.

When travelling south *from Carriacou to Grenada* it is quite possible to make Saint George's Harbour in Grenada in a day if you leave Tyrrel Bay early in the morning, but once you reach the west coast of Grenada there will be little wind so expect to motor sail. Some yachts sail down Grenada's east, windward coast to the anchorage in the south of the island in Prickly Bay, but off the windward side of Grenada the Atlantic seas can be large and the trade winds strong. If you attempt this route sail inside Bird Island but make sure you leave all the other islands to starboard.

Charts:
British Admiralty: 2872 General
French: 3206 General
USA: 25482 General
Imray Iolaire: B31 Bequia to Carriacou, B32 Carriacou to Grenada, B311 Canouan to Carriacou

Airport
There is an inter-island airstrip a mile south west of Hillsborough on Carriacou.

GRENADA

The history of this most beautiful of all the Windward Islands is one of conflicts, which began in the pre-Columbian period when the Arawaks were ousted by the Caribs, and most recently in 1983 when the United States marines invaded Grenada and overthrew a pro-Cuban administration. Columbus sighted Grenada in 1498 on his third voyage to the Caribbean and named the island Asuncion, because it was the day of the vigil of the Feast of Assumption, the church feast commemorating the reception into heaven of the Virgin Mary. Amerigo Vespucci named the island Mayo but by about 1525 the Spanish map makers were calling the island Grenada.

If Columbus had landed he would have found Grenada firmly in the hands of the Caribs. In the early seventeenth century, although technically a Spanish colony, Britain landed settlers on the island, but they were beaten back by the Caribs as were the first French settlers who next tried to land. But in 1650 the French Governor of Martinique landed a strong force and drove the Caribs back to the north of the island where, rather than surrender to the French soldiers, they jumped to their deaths in the sea. The hill is still known as Morne des Sauteurs - Leaper's Hill.

Despite attempts by Saint Vincent Caribs to avenge their fellow tribesmen, the French colonists held the island until it was ceded to Britain in 1763 by the Treaty of Paris. The Treaty marked the end of the Seven Years' War between Britain and France and, along with Grenada, Britain gained the Grenadines, Saint Vincent, Dominica and Tobago. War broke out again between Britain and France in 1776 when France gave assistance to Britain's breakaway American colonies, and the French recaptured the island in 1779. Grenada was returned to the British by the 1783 Treaty of Versailles and remained a British colony until the island became fully independent in 1974.

The general demise of the West Indian plantations coupled with the abolition of slavery reduced the power and importance of most of the Caribbean islands during the nineteenth century. But Grenada, a rich and fertile land, continued to prosper, exporting cocoa, nutmeg and bananas to such an extent that it became known as the 'Spice Island' - it is the only spice-producing island in the western hemisphere. Grenada was one of the wealthiest of all the British Caribbean colonies until it was devastated by Hurricane Janet in 1955.

In 1951 Eric M Gairy helped organise a general strike and led a popular protest movement. He and his party, the Grenada United Labour Party, swept to power in the same year, and for the next 28 years Eric Gairy more or less ruled Grenada. Liked by the old, hated by the young, the increasingly despotic Gairy eventually had his authority challenged by a number of opposition groups who united to form the New Jewel Movement. In 1979 an almost bloodless coup brought the New Jewel Movement into power and a People's Revolutionary Government was installed with its leader Maurice Bishop and its second in command Bernard Coard. The constitution was suspended, the press were controlled and the People's Revolutionary Army given the same powers of arrest and search as the police. The Cubans were invited to the island and, largely through their efforts, an international airport was built at Point Saline in the south of the island. But Bishop and Coard clashed, and Bishop was taken prisoner and executed along with half his cabinet.

The United States, anxious to avoid another communist stronghold in the Caribbean, especially one so close to South America, invaded Grenada in 1983 - probably with the support of most of the Grenadians. Today Grenada is politically stable and tourism is once again playing an important role in the island's economy: the Cuban-built international airport regularly flies in tourists from New York and London. Grenada now has a population of around 100 000, with some 9 000 inhabitants residing in the island's capital, Saint George's.

Grenada is re-emerging as the most important yachting centre in the southern Caribbean. Until recently it was only possible to overnight in Saint George's Harbour and Prickly Bay in the south, but now the southern coast has been reopened and cruising boats can once again visit its picturesque, well-sheltered anchorages - which

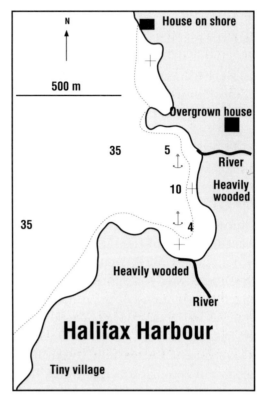

include the important hurricane hole at Port Egremont. With the present government's positive attitude, yachts can visit the island for nothing and stay for as long as they wish. The first anchorage when coming down the west coast from the north is tiny Halifax Harbour, a useful overnight spot for yachts voyaging to or from the north.

Halifax Harbour

When travelling north *from Grenada to Carriacou* the trip can be a tough beat and some skippers (although this is becoming less popular) make an overnight stop in Halifax Harbour before setting out early in the morning to tackle the passage. Motor sail north along the west coast of Grenada from Halifax or Saint George's Harbour keeping about a quarter of a mile offshore. When you leave the north of Grenada, close to David Point, head straight for Diamond Island as there is often a very strong, westerly current. If you have no engine it might pay to beat right up to Ronde Isle before setting out into the channel.

Approach

You should only approach the harbour only by day, and this small sheltered double bay is easy to miss. Coming *from the north*, after Black Bay Point the coast leads away to Halifax Harbour. The best landmark is a pink concrete house built on the shore, and the entrance to the harbour is about a quarter of a mile south of this house. There is a house half hidden in the trees on the hill on the north side of the harbour.

Approaching *from the south*, keep close to the shore after Boismorice Point and the entrance is just north of a small village. Look out for the overgrown house, and if you come to the pink house you have come too far north .

Anchorage

Anchor in the north east corner of the outer bay, off the small river, in about 4 metres depth in good holding sandy mud. The bottom comes up quickly and there are rocks close to the shore. You can anchor in the southern, inner bay in sandy mud. The bottom also comes up quickly to about 1.80 metres and there are isolated rocks.

Ashore

Nothing.

After Halifax Harbour the coast runs south west to Boismorice or Molinière Point and then south east. The large oil storage tanks at Grand Mal are very conspicuous when travelling to Saint George's from the north.

Saint George's Harbour

Saint George's is the capital of Grenada and is one of the most picturesque towns in the southern Caribbean. Saint George's is built on a steep hill and the narrow streets wind round ancient, soft-red brick houses whose walls were brought to the island long ago as sailing ship ballast.

The entrance to the harbour is between two distinct headlands and there are two anchorages, one off the town in the Carenage bay and the other in a sheltered lagoon. The lagoon is a possible hurricane hole.

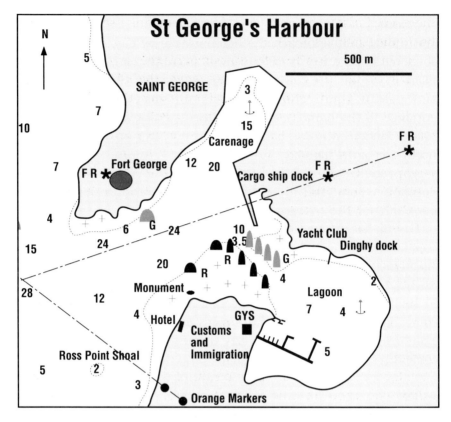

Approach

Approach by day although, in theory, Saint George's Harbour is one of the best lit harbours in the southern Caribbean. As you approach *from the north* you will see the town stretching up the hill and its three churches - two with red tin roofs. The harbour entrance lies south of Fort George. There is a sectored light on the north west corner of the Fort (F R 188 ft 15M: visible 56° - 151° True).

Approaching *from the south* the only danger after Point Saline is Long Point Shoal. Steer for the conspicuous oil storage tanks at Grand Mal and when the entrance bears about east turn to starboard for Saint George's Harbour.

Grenada's buoys are IALA System B (that is red right returning) so when you enter the harbour leave the red buoys to starboard. There is plenty of depth on the approach for yachts - the orange-painted daytime transits are for large cargo ships. On the southern headland you will see a distinctive hotel.

Once inside the harbour on the starboard bow you will see a statue, a monument to the hospitality shown by the people of Grenada to the rescued passengers and crew of an Italian cruise ship that caught fire in the harbour in 1961.

In front of you as you enter the harbour is the cargo ship dock and the bay off to port is the Carenage where there is an anchorage. However, in the Carenage the water is dirty, the air is hot and windless, there is much local boat movement and the surrounding roads are noisy with traffic. The best anchorage is in the lagoon. Aim for the centre of the cargo ship dock and turn to starboard when you can see down a buoyed and staked channel (red to starboard when entering) that is dredged to about 3.5 metres. Keep to the middle of the channel and enter the lagoon.

If you have to enter at night the green and red buoys are supposedly lit (Q G; Q R) and you can line up the transit on the big ship leading lights (F R) on 080° Magnetic, which passes over the southern end of the cargo ship dock. At night turn to port and anchor in the Carenage in depths of 5 to 10 metres in good holding black mud. At sun-up move to the lagoon.

Anchorage
Drop the anchor in the lagoon in depths of 3 to 8 metres in yellowish water over good holding black sticky mud. The lagoon is well sheltered and possibly a good refuge in a hurricane, providing it is not too crowded.

Alongside and Ashore
The Grenada Yacht Club is on the hill that overlooks the channel into the lagoon. The club has a bar, showers, fresh water (fill your own container) and welcomes visiting yachts. The Club owns a rickety 10-ton, 2 metre railway haul but the last time I was there the cradle and winch looked very rusty. A dinghy dock is situated in the north of the lagoon, next to the railway haul, but as there have been some thefts recently make sure you lock the outboard motor and the oars to the dinghy. Grenada Yacht Club organises an Easter regatta race between Trinidad and Grenada, and cruising yachts are always welcome to join in the fun.

In the southern end of the lagoon are the broken down jetties of the Grenada Yacht Services (GYS) that are about to be replaced (although this has been 'about to happen' since 1985). You can go alongside these rotting pontoons and, as their state of repair is so bad, the rates are reasonable. Water and electricity are available on the jetty. A 230-ton railway haul is tucked away in the north west corner of the lagoon, but it is generally being used by local boats. GYS has a fuel dock, a chandlery, and a run down machine and woodwork shop. On the lagoon road are McIntyre Bros who will help with any diesel problem and the GYS complex has a bar and a restaurant - often closed in the low season. Scuba diving can be arranged through HMC Diving at the complex. At the moment GYS has a general air of decay and disrepair, and this once thriving yachting centre has yet to recover its former glory.

It is sometimes possible to hail a water taxi to carry you to the town, otherwise take the dinghy and moor at either Food Fair supermarket, opposite the north end of the cargo ship dock, or a little further south on the west side of the Carenage at the new dock at Delicious Landing - where skippers may eat free for five or more in their party.

It is a short taxi ride or a 20 minute walk to town from the lagoon. In Saint George's there are some excellent restaurants, as well as supermarkets, banks, a vegetable market, post office, and the Best Little Liquor Store in Town which sells duty free alcohol and delivers to GYS or Prickly Bay. Huggins at the Carenage, who will recharge gas bottles, and Hubbards Hardware on Wharf Road, are two useful shops. Two interesting walks, with wonderful views, are along Church Street to the cemetery and the road off Young Street to Fort George. Tours worth booking are to Grand Etang lake, the Annandale waterfall and Le Morne des Sauteurs.

Customs and Immigration

These are situated in the GYS complex. The hours are 0800 to 1145, then from 1300 to 1545. Overtime is payable between 1145 and 1300 and after 1545, and on Saturdays, Sundays and Public Holidays. When you sail to the south of the island from Saint George's you have to notify the authorities. Saint George's is one of three points of entry into Grenada - the other two are at Prickly Bay in the south and Grenville on the windward side of the island.

The lagoon in Saint George's Harbour can be hot and airless and the water is cloudy and dirty, so once you have reprovisioned you might prefer to sail off to the superb Grand Anse beach, which is the first bay south of the harbour.

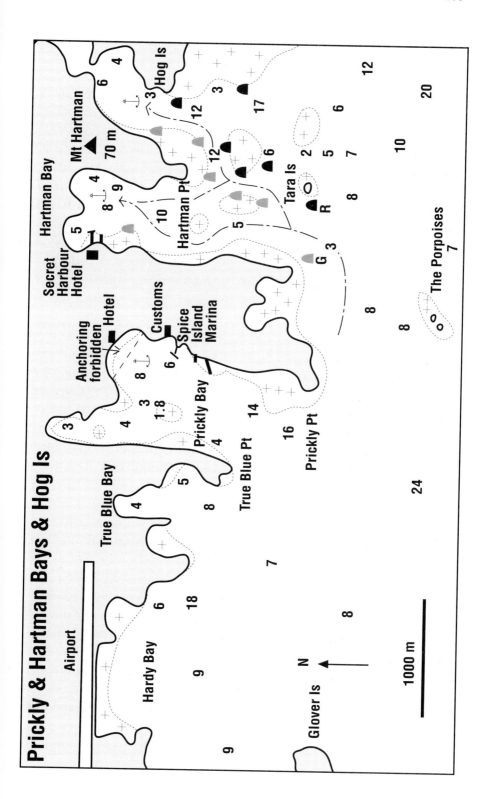

Prickly & Hartman Bays & Hog Is

Grand Anse

The anchorage faces two miles of uninterrupted golden sands and in the summer months, when there is little northerly swell, it is one of the great Caribbean anchorages.

Approach
From the north give the shoal north west of Ross Point a good clearance, especially if you draw any more than 2 metres. Head for the centre of the bay. *From the south* give the shoal off Long Point a wide berth and as there are shoals in the south of the bay; keep to its centre.

Anchorage
Anchor in a depth of about 3 metres in good holding sand in front of the Ramada Renaissance Hotel. To the north is the Coconut Beach French Restaurant which is a good place to leave the dinghy.

Ashore
Dinghies have to be left on the beach as there are no docks. The Coconut Beach French Restaurant, Spice Island Inn, Ramada Renaissance and other hotels offer entertainment and reasonably expensive dining. Opposite the Ramada Renaissance is a large shopping centre with boutiques, supermarkets and cheaper restaurants.

South of Grand Anse Bay is little **Morne Rouge Bay**. The small anchorage is tucked in behind Long Point and to the east of Long Point Shoal in Morne Rouge Bay. One or two yachts can drop anchor in depths of between 2 to 3 metres in fair-holding, weed-covered sand. The bottom comes up very quickly as you approach the bay. You can sail between Long Point Shoal and Long Point.

The anchorages on the south coast of Grenada are as numerous as they are beautiful. The area should be approached with care as the coast is exposed to the trade winds, especially in the summer months when the winds are more southerly. When travelling *from the north* to Point Saline, the south west point of Grenada, a real danger is Long Point Shoal which is unmarked and lies about half a mile off the coast. As you approach Point Saline take bearings off the oil tanks at Grand Mal and off the end of Point Saline to continuously check your position. When you round the point be prepared to reef the main as you will be hard on the wind and the heavy Atlantic swell will be running.

Prickly Bay

About two miles east of Point Saline is Prickly Bay. The anchorage in Prickly Bay is truly a classical Caribbean anchorage - picturesque, breezy, safe and secluded. It is becoming increasingly popular as a point of departure for Venezuela and South America when yachts head south in the summer time to avoid the Caribbean hurricane season.

Approach

From the north round Point Saline which is supposedly lit (Q (9) 15s 7M) and expect to see low flying aircraft from the new airport's runway. Prickly Point, the eastern headland into Prickly Bay, is the furthest visible headland. Most yachts motor sail the short distance from Point Saline to Prickly Bay.

Approaching *from the south*, perhaps arriving just before dawn from Venezuela, Trinidad or Tobago, the light south of Morne Rouge Bay can be seen from a long way out, and is a good landmark for Prickly Bay. It has an unusual characteristic (Fl (2+1) 20s 357ft 18 M). By day, the yacht masts at the head are conspicuous. Be sure to give the Porpoises, an unmarked group of rocks that lie about a mile south of Prickly Point, a wide berth as they are just above the surface and, because of the Atlantic swell, the rocks are sometimes difficult to see. Glover Island is a useful landmark.

When entering Prickly Bay keep to the centre of the bay as both the east and west shores are reef strewn. Avoid a small, usually unmarked, coral reef that is in the centre of the bay, almost opposite the pontoon berths of Spice Island Marine Services on the east side of the bay. The reef is hard to identify as it is usually surrounded by anchored yachts. You can swim in the bay although the water is sometimes not very clear.

Anchorage

Drop the anchor in depths of between 3 and 7 metres; the bottom is hard sand and sometimes difficult to penetrate. Do not anchor closer than 300 metres to the shore in the north east corner of the bay as the area is reserved for bathers and water sports. There is also an anchorage in a small bay that runs off the north west corner of Prickly Bay, but approach with care as the water is cloudy and there is a shoal in the middle of the bay. This anchorage in depths of around 3 metres may offer shelter from the unpleasant swell that sometimes enters Prickly Bay in the summer months.

Alongside and Ashore

In the middle of the east bank Spice Island Marine Services have become the hub of yachting in Grenada - since the demise of GYS at Saint George's Harbour. They have a small, well maintained marina with some 25 berths, each with electricity and fresh water. A fuel and fresh water dock is situated on the main pontoon.

Spice Island Marine Services has a 35-ton travel lift and you can work on your boat in a clean, airy boatyard that overlooks the bay. A chandlery, a sail loft, a small supermarket, a laundry and a mechanic are all to be found within 500 metres of the yard. There are telephones, a telex and a poste restante (Yacht<>, Poste Restante, Spice Island Marine Services, Box 449, Saint George's, Grenada, West Indies). The Boatyard restaurant also has a bar which is a meeting point for cruising people. In the north east corner of the bay the Calabash Hotel rents dinghies and windsurfers and serves first class food. Behind the hotel, a short walk along the road, is an English style pub - the Red Crab. The Horseshoe Beach Hotel is another first class restaurant at the south east corner of the bay and only a short dinghy ride away from the anchorage. The hotel organises scuba dives (VHF ch 16) and has a dinghy dock. From Prickly Bay Saint George's is reachable by bus or taxi and you are close to the international airport.

Customs and Immigration

The offices are to the north of the small marina. Prickly Bay is a point of entry and the officials work the same hours as those in Saint George's Harbour. They will give you permission to visit other anchorages in the south of the island and, if you are voyaging north, the anchorages in Carriacou.

All the anchorages to the east of Prickly Bay require some degree of caution as there are only a few buoys and one cove tends to look like another, especially when approaching *from the south*. It is always best to enter the bays when the sun is high; do not attempt to enter late in the afternoon. The first anchorage east after Prickly Bay is in Mount Hartman Bay or Secret Harbour. Since the Moorings organisation has laid a set of buoys to their Secret Harbour Hotel the entrance to this bay has been much improved.

Mount Hartman Bay (Secret Harbour)

This a well sheltered anchorage with a superb hotel and restaurant which has its own dinghy dock.

Approach
From Prickly Bay turn to port and pass inside The Porpoises, a group of rocks which stand about 1 metre above water and are difficult to see. Ahead is Tara Island, a tiny coral patch about 2 metres high, and the first two Moorings organisation buoys. Leave the red buoy to starboard and travel up the middle of the marked channel that passes half way between Tara Island and the shore. You can either turn to port leaving the first green buoy on the *starboard* bow and carefully follow the reef that runs up the west coast of the bay, or continue along the buoyed passage and after passing the third green buoy turn to *port* and enter Hartman Bay. Both routes miss the two coral reefs that lie in the centre of the entrance to Hartman Bay.

Anchorage
Anchor anywhere in the bay although most yachts anchor off the docks in front of the Secret Harbour Hotel in the north west corner of the bay. Anchor in depths of 4 to 9 metres; the holding is good in sandy mud. The water is not always very clear.

Ashore
Secret Harbour is one of the most beautiful resorts in Grenada. A new dock has been constructed just south of the hotel and there are over a dozen charter boats already operating from this complex. There is an excellent restaurant ashore and the possibility of obtaining fresh water from the new dock.

Just to the east of Mount Hartman Point is Hog Island, once a deserted anchorage but now, because of the Moorings organisation buoys, easily accessible.

Hog Island

Although the approach has recently been buoyed, Hog Island is still one of the most isolated and enchanting of Grenada's southern anchorages.

Approach

The easiest approach is *from Mount Hartman Bay*. Identify the green buoy off Mount Hartman Point and, leaving this and the next green buoys to port, head up into the anchorage which is on the north west corner of Hog Island in a small creek. The shoals south of the island are marked with red buoys which, as you are entering, must be left to starboard. Approaching *from seaward* wait until Hartman Point bears about 023° Magnetic and lines up with the peak of Mount Hartman. Carefully sail this course to enter the Moorings organisation's buoyed channel. The first starboard hand, red Moorings buoy is south west of Tara Island.

Anchorage

Anchor in depths of 2 to 3 metres; the bottom is good holding muddy sand.

Ashore

Nothing but wonderful walks and wild nature. There is a fine beach in the south.

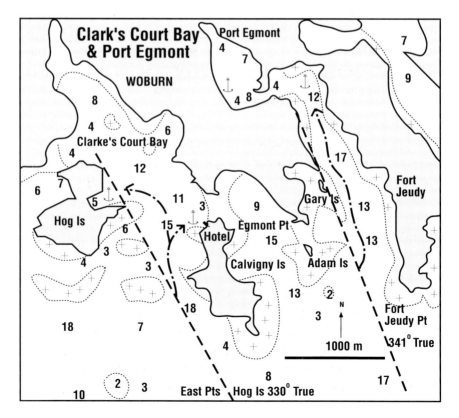

Clark's Court Bay & Port Egmont

Clarke's Court Bay

The next bay east of Hog Island is Clarke's Court Bay - a huge bay that contains many picturesque creeks and coves. Because of the dangerous unmarked reefs the sun must be high when you enter.

Approach
Coming *from the Hog Island anchorage* the safest route is to return along the Moorings organisation's buoyed channel to the open sea. Sail eastwards and identify Calvigny Island and head towards its shores. *From seaward* the two east points of Hog Island line up on 330° True. Come in on this bearing but leave the shoals that the bearing passes over to port. Keep close to the west shore of Calvigny Island but watch out for the rocks that extend some distance off its southern tip. Reefs extend a long way to the south east of Hog Island.

Anchorage
In the north west of Calvigny Island you can anchor by the dock that is in front of the hotel. Anchor in depths of between 3 and 5 metres in good holding weed-covered mud. There is also a good anchorage in the north east corner of Hog Island. Some yachts travel up to the north east head of Clarke's Court Bay and anchor off the jetty at the village of Woburn, but do this only in good light and clear water as there are dangerous shoals as you head up the bay.

Ashore
A few basics at Woburn where buses run to Saint George's. Calvigny Island is worth exploring. East of Calvigny is the best hurricane hole in Grenada and in this guide; the enclosed lagoon of Port Egmont.

Port Egmont

Approach
The entrance is easy, but enter only when the sun is high. Coming *from Clarke's Court Bay* it is best to return to the open sea about a mile offshore. Head a short distance east, giving the shoals south of Calvigny Island a good clearance, until you see the eastern end of Gary Island and the eastern shore of Point Egmont line up on 341° True. Keep just east of this line heading towards, but not too close to,

the shores off Fort Jeudy where there is some building taking place. Keeping to the east side of the bay work your way north west to its head. Beware of the long shoal that stretches north east away from the land and is less than half a mile north of Gary Island.

Anchorage

Anchor in the north east corner of the bay, or enter the completely sheltered inner creek which makes such a good hurricane hole. Here you can anchor in depths of 4 to 8 metres in good holding black mud.

Ashore

Nothing but fishing huts.

There are other bays to explore such as **Calvigny Harbour** and **Westerhall Bay**. Both entrances require caution, a high sun and settled conditions.

Charts

British Admiralty: 2821 General, 2830 St George's Harbour
French: 3273 General
USA: 25481 General
Imray Iolaire: B32 Grenada to Carriacou

Radio Station, Frequency and Times of Weather Bulletin

Radio Grenada: 535 kHz

Airport

International Airport at Point Saline. Tel 444 4101

The tethered pig roots for shell fish. Isla Iguana, Los Testigos, Venezuela

VENEZUELA

Columbus was the first European to land on Venezuela; he landed in 1498 shortly after making a landfall on the island of Trinidad at the end of his third voyage across the Atlantic. Voyaging west along the southern coast of Trinidad he dropped anchor in what is now known as Erin Bay and then sailed through the narrow passage between Trinidad and South America into the huge Gulf of Paria to anchor behind Icacos Point in what is now known as Columbus Bay.

As he was weighing anchor a huge wave roared through the passage between Trinidad and South America, possibly caused by some volcanic disturbance, and after nearly losing his flagship Columbus named the passage La Boca de la Sierpie - the Serpent's Mouth. He sailed north through the Gulf of Paria and landed on Venezuela at a small bay at the south of the Paria Peninsula. It is difficult to identify the exact site of this first European landing in South America but Samuel Morison, an authority on Columbus, suggested it might have been Ensenada Yacua, although equally likely spots would be Ensenada Cariaquita or the bay in front of the town of Puerto Macuro. The local Indians informed Columbus that the region was known as Paria, and Columbus claimed the newly discovered land for Spain - it was later to become the Republic of Venezuela.

Columbus probably sailed out of the Gulf of Paria through the Boca Grande, and because of the disturbed waters in the passage he named the northern entrance to the Gulf of Paria the Bocas Del Dragon - the Dragon's Mouth. Columbus sighted the distant island of Grenada and continued in a north westerly direction towards Los Testigos islands before reaching back towards Venezuela. He observed Margarita Island, which he named after the Infanta Margarita of

Austria, but did not land. He did not stay on the Venezuelan coast but set sail for Hispaniola.

It was Alonso de Ojeda, a caravel captain on Columbus' second voyage, who was the first European to land on Margarita Island. In 1499 Ojeda led the next European expedition after Columbus to the Venezuelan coast, and after landing on Margarita Ojeda sailed further west to discover the islands of Aruba, Bonaire and Curacao. He entered Lake Maracaibo and, on seeing Indian villages built on stilts, named the country Venezuela - Little Venice. Ojeda soon discovered that the sea south of Margarita, especially around Cubagua Island, was rich in pearl-bearing oysters and this stretch of the Venezuelan coast later became known as the Pearl Coast.

Spanish settlers arrived in the early 1500s on the island of Cubagua, just five miles south of Margarita Island, and called their settlement Nueva Cadiz. The settlers, soon exhausting the supplies of Cubaguan pearls, moved to the mainland where they built farms and raised cattle. Venezuela remained under Spanish control for the next three centuries and the settlers farmed and ranched, profitably exporting tobacco, cocoa, salt and wheat. In the late 1700s the prosperous Venezuelan settlers demanded free trade with other nations but Spain, the colonial master, required that all Venezuela's produce be sold to Spain or its colonies. Simon Bolivar led the country to independence in a bloody struggle that ended in 1821 and decimated half the population. However, free Venezuela was unable to reach political stability, and over 20 constitutions and 50 armed revolts followed independence - it was not until 1947 that democratic elections were held. Juan Gomez was elected president in 1910 and did much to modernise Venezuela, but he governed either directly or indirectly as a dictator, ruthlessly using the army to control the population. He died in 1935 after amassing an enormous personal fortune.

Vast oil deposits were discovered in 1917 and since then the economy has largely been dependent on oil: Venezuela is still one of the world's largest producers and suppliers. Oil was nationalised in 1976 and the country is now trying to diversify its economy and produce diamonds, aluminium and gold and other metals of which there are rich deposits. In the 1980s oil revenue fell seriously, the country's foreign debt increased and there were food riots. Today the country is politically stable and tourism is coming to the mainland. There are some 16 million people living in Venezuela. The capital is

Caracas and the main port is Maracaibo which is situated on the north west shore of Lake Maracaibo. A waterway was built in 1956 connecting Lake Maracaibo to the Gulf of Venezuela, but as Lake Maracaibo is exclusively dedicated to oil production it is not a place for yachts.

Venezuela, like many South American countries, is a land of contrasts: from uninhabited golden-sanded islands, surrounded by clear turquoise water, to filthy cities and oil stained beaches; from tropical forest to desert, in just a few hundred miles of coastline; and from extreme wealth to extreme poverty. The Venezuelans are warm and friendly, the offshore islands are spectacular, probably the best in the Caribbean (especially Los Testigos and Los Roques), and in the interior, which is readily and cheaply accessible by air, you can ski in the Andes or visit the world's highest waterfall, the Angel Falls or, from the port of Cumana, explore the deep, eight mile long Guachero cave. However, there are only a few yachting facilities (none on most of the small islands); the nearer to mainland Venezuela you sail the greener, cloudier and more oily the water; there is thievery and corruption; the paperwork for entering and clearing is horrendous; and the winds are light to non-existent along the eastern mainland coast (which is an advantage for an east bound yacht with a good auxiliary engine). Nevertheless each summer the number of cruising yachts visiting Venezuela's north east coast and its offshore islands is steadily increasing.

The Venezuelan currency devaluation in 1983 made Venezuela suddenly very popular with British, American and French cruising yachts, but by 1990 prices had risen, although the country is still relatively cheap (for example a good meal in a first class restaurant costs around $15 US per person). Apart from the cheapness, cruising people enjoy, and are always on the lookout for, new countries and cultures to explore and Venezuela is markedly different from the Caribbean islands But perhaps the most important reason for Venezuela's increasing popularity is that it is out of the hurricane belt, although it can be affected by occasional heavy swells and tropical depressions. Hurricane Hugo roared its destructive way through Guadeloupe and the Caribbean in 1989. The following year in June and July, the beginning of the hurricane season, there were hundreds of yachts of all nationalities hurrying south along the island chain towards Grenada - the departure point for Venezuela.

A classical two to three month Venezuelan summer tour starting and finishing at Grenada would be to sail from Grenada with the north east trades to the offshore islands of Los Testigos, Margarita, perhaps Blanquilla and Tortuga, or even as as far west as Los Roques, before returning by sailing eastwards (probably motor sailing), via Cubagua and Coche Islands, along the northern Venezuelan coast against the very light easterly winds. If there were time it would be worth including a short visit to Trinidad and then Tobago before sailing back to Grenada. Most yachts, however, sail directly back to Grenada (or Martinique via Los Testigos) from a point on the northern Venezuelan coast that lies just west of the Bocas Del Dragon.

Before you arrive in Venezuela you will need a visa, and one of the easiest places to obtain one is Fort de France, Martinique. The Venezuelan embassy is on the Route de Didier that runs through the hills overlooking Fort de France. The embassy is open from 0900 to 1200 each weekday and to get there you can take a bus from the depot near the cemetery in Fort de France. The visa costs about $20 US per person (the embassy accepts only American dollars). Take your passport, two passport photographs and the ship's papers. If you are lucky the passport will be returned stamped with the visa the next day. You can also obtain a visa in Grenada where the embassy is located on Archibald Avenue, St George's, and is open from 1000 to 1300. The visa can take up to a week to obtain, especially in the summer months.

Venezuela is administratively divided into states and you need a Zarpe (cruising permit) for each of the states. When you arrive in each state you will be issued with a Zarpe by the authorities. Before you set out for Los Testigos islands, the first classical Venezuelan anchorage, make sure you fill up with fuel, fresh water and fresh vegetables as they are non-existent on these islands. Most yachts set out from Prickly Bay in the south of Grenada in the early evening to arrive off Los Testigos at sun-up.

Los Testigos

These are some of the most enchanting islands in the Caribbean and I shall always remember the morning after a fast, rolling night passage that led us to the main anchorage behind Testigo Grande. After breakfast, tired but content, we lazily swam ashore to be greeted by three, young, beautiful Venezuelan women, daughters of the local

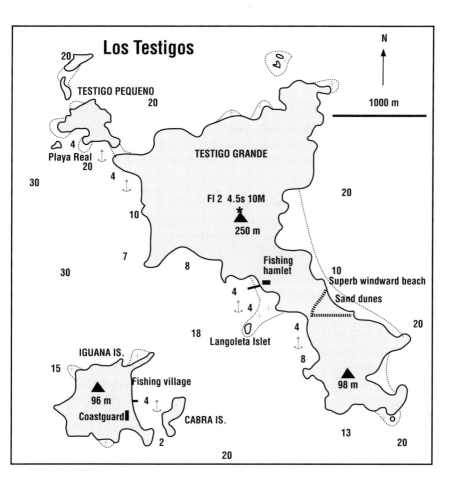

fishermen. They splashed and jumped around us as we rested in the shallows, our bodies half in and half out of the clear warm water that just rippled the white, sun-bleached coral sands. They spoke to us in Spanish and, before we could attempt to reply, they ran up the beach and disappeared into the palm trees. Soon they returned to offer us drinks from freshly opened coconuts and wild apricots that felt warm and tasted sweet. We sat under the shade of the palm trees - we had little Spanish, they had no English - drinking, eating, smiling and laughing. The morning passed as a timeless series of magic moments and was one of the many unforgettable, enchanting days I have experienced when cruising.

There are some 100 inhabitants on Los Testigos - fishing people who mostly live on La Iguana (Iguana Island), the only island which has an electricity generator. The waters around Los Testigos, although not always clear because of the Orinoco current, abound with fish, so on your way over trail a line, or exchange fish with the local fishermen for the fresh fruit and vegetables you carried from Grenada.

Approach

This is not easy, mainly because of the unknown strength of the powerful west going current makes it difficult to determine an exact position. The current can run up to a maximum of four knots, although it is usually around two to two and a half knots, and the direction is erratic although always with a westerly component. Further, the light on Isla Testigo Grande (Fl 4.5s, 815ft 10M) rarely works, or if it does, it is not visible at its supposed range of 10 miles.

It is best to leave Prickly Bay just before dusk, and keep the speed down to arrive around dawn, assuming some 30 knots of north west current and a total rhumb line voyage of about 90 miles. This voyage is one of the few Caribbean trips described in this guide where a satellite navigator is of great use; without one, try to sail in company and use your VHF. I would aim for the southern tip of Isla Rajada, but if in any doubt of your position heave to before dawn, shoot the stars at dawn if you are handy with a sextant, and wait for a sighting of the islands. If you are completely unsure of your position a good trick is to head well south of Los Testigos to pick up on the depth sounder the large bank (8 to 10 metres) that extends about 15 miles south to south east of the island. When you have sorted out your position, and the different islands, steer for the southern tip of Testigo Grande - it is quite possible to steer between Isla Conejo and Isla Rajada.

There are a number of anchorages around Los Testigos, but the usual first stop is on Isla Testigo Grande, north of the little Langoleta Islet and across the channel from the settlement on La Iguana. You will see the masts of the yachts at anchor behind the little offshore islet as you round the southern end of Testigo Grande, but do not be tempted to head between the islet and the mainland as the passage is too shallow for a deep-keeled yacht.

If you end up north of Testigo Grande, leave Testigo Pequeno and its offlying islets well to port, before turning into the channel between Testigo Grande and La (Isla) Iguana. The current can run north westerly at up to two and half knots in this channel.

Anchorage

Anchor in depths of about 4 metres behind the islet in good holding sand and in front of the few fishermen's houses and their dock. This,

like most of the anchorages on Los Testigos, can be affected by swell
so a second anchor from the stern to hold the bow on to the waves is
sometimes effective. You can moor your dinghy at the fishermen's
dock, although it is just as easy to drag it up the beach.

There are several other anchorages on Los Testigos:
Isla Iguana: Moor in front of the village or behind Isla Cabra. There
is a dinghy dock.
**Between Testigo Pequeno and Testigo Grande off Playa
Real:** This is the second most popular anchorage. There is a sandy
spit connecting Testigo Grande and Testigo Pequeno and yachts
anchor behind the spit. The anchorage is breezy; if you tuck yourself
in there is less swell and the water is clear and about 4 metres deep.
Some yachts anchor off the beach north or south of the spit.
Testigo Grande, south of the sand dunes: In the south east
corner of the bay, south of Langoleta Islet and just south of the huge
sand dune that has blown across from the windward side of the
island, there is a rather airless but calm anchorage in about 8 metres.

Ashore
There is nothing to buy but much fresh fish, lobsters and the
occasional beer to barter for. The windward side of Testigo Grande has
a huge deserted sandy beach where swimming in the large waves that
crash ashore is a once in a lifetime experience. Leave the dinghy just
south of the large dune that has blown through to the leeward side of
the island and climb over the top of the dune to the beach. It will be
hot so take fresh water and shoes (the sand burns the soles of your
feet) as it is a short but stiff climb.

Customs and Immigration
When you arrive hoist the Q flag. The local Coastguards are situated
on Isla Iguana up the hill inside a fibreglass cabin. They zoom around
in a motor boat or a local fishing boat and will ask you to report to
the station on Iguana. Take the yacht across, or if you have a reliable
outboard motor, go by dinghy - the current is strong between the two
islands. The Coastguards will inspect the ship's papers and the crew's
passports. There are the usual forms to fill in but that is all; the real
business of entering Venezuela takes place in Pampatar on Margarita.
    Isla de Margarita is Venezuela's holiday island and Porlamar is a
duty-free port where the tourists from the mainland and other parts

of South America come to spend their bolivars. There are luxurious, top class resorts and shops but they are not the rule; most boutiques sell cheap, poor quality goods - but there are bargains to be had. The oysters are very cheap and of the highest quality and, if you are lucky, there is something like a one in fifty chance of finding a pearl.

Pampatar

Pampatar is the entry port for the island of Margarita and the Republic of Venezuela and is situated on Margarita's south east coast.

Approach

The passage *from Los Testigos* to Pampatar on Margarita Island is an easy downwind sail of about 50 miles. Do not forget to allow for the north westerly current - if you sail close to the small islet La Sola you have been swept too far north. Aim for Punta Ballena; the Los Frailes Islands stand out from the shore, and at a distance the high mountains in the middle of Margarita will help fix your position. The next headland south of Punta Ballena, Punta Moreno, appears from some way out as a separate island. Punta Ballena is to the south of the central mountains. If you are sailing in *from a southerly direction* Isla Blanco is a good landmark - and it does look white.

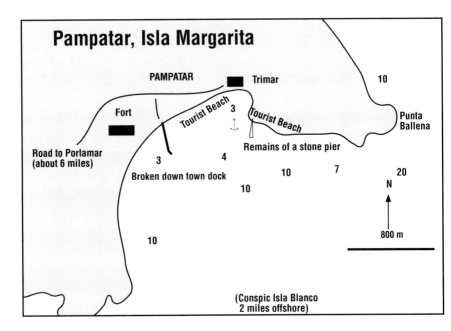

Pampatar, Isla Margarita

The anchorage is tucked away behind Punta Bellana and, as it is open to the south and can therefore be unpleasant in any southerly swell. It is often crowded in summer.

Anchorage

After Punta Ballena there is plenty of water close to the shore. Pass a small beach, a stone pier and turn to starboard towards the brokendown town pier. Go as close to the beach and near the restaurant Trimar as the other anchored yachts will let you, and drop the anchor in depths of between 3 to 5 metres in hard, blackish sand that is sometimes difficult to penetrate with a CQR.

Ashore

You can leave your dinghy on the beach by the Trimar restaurant where, for a small sum, it will be looked after from 0900 to midnight. You could leave the dinghy at the brokendown town dock but at best the local children will fill it with sand and water. There are restaurants all along the beach and during the weekend there is a real party atmosphere - try the oysters which are cheap and especially good when smoked over wood fires on the beach.

Most visiting yacht people tend to congregate in the Trimar bar/restaurant which offers free showers. Pampatar has a bakery and a few small supermarkets; the largest is situated on the road to Porlamar. A cheap, regular bus service runs to Porlamar. The fort is worth a visit and the beach is quite clean.

Margarita Yacht Services (VHF ch 68) located in the centre of Pampatar beach makes sun awnings, and they carry out wood and fibreglass repairs and can repair alternators, starter motors and diesel injectors. Shore Base Yacht Services, which is run by an American and a Venezuelan, is found behind the Trimar and they also stand by on VHF ch 68. They will act as a bureau de change and help you with almost anything you need: island tours, fax, visa extensions, telex, diesel mechanic, charts, diesel, fresh water by the container, new dinghies and outboard motors, a laundry and an English book exchange. Best of all they will help with entering.

Customs and Immigration

For a fee, which is excellent value (about $20 US), Shore Base Yacht Services will enter you into Venezuela and help you on your way. You could need help, especially if you speak no Spanish, as you are supposed to enter and clear from each of the major ports on the Venezuelan coast. If you do not use Shore Base Yacht Services put aside a day and be prepared to return to the yacht possibly overcharged and with a lot of stamped, shuffled and signed papers. You will have to visit the Immigration, National Guard, Customs and the Port Captain, and if you do wish to stop at ports other than the major ones you have to have permission to visit them - Todos Puntas Intermedios has to be stamped on your papers. But then, what is a day lost in the life of a cruising yacht?

Just west of Pampatar is Porlamar, a bustling modern city, full of skyscrapers. Porlamar is a duty free port, with an enormous number of shops selling so called 'duty-free bargains'. But although many shops sell goods with internationally known labels much of the merchandise is poor-quality 'seconds'.

A government subsidy encouraged many yachts to go to Venezuela specifically to buy outboard motors, but the subsidy has recently been withdrawn and outboards are as expensve here as they are in the rest of the Caribbean. However, anywhere in Venezuela diesel fuel and engine oil are incredibly cheap, but the quality and the cleanliness of the fuel can be very poor. Once in Martinique I saw a diesel tank from a yacht that had spent a year cruising Venezuela. The 70 gallon tank was three quarters full of thick grey sludge - it took a week to clean it - so if you buy Venezuelan fuel make sure you add a powerful biotoxin to kill bacterial sludge.

Porlamar

Porlamar is situated in the north west corner of a huge, five mile wide bay, the Bahia La Mar.

Approach
The entrance to the bay, which is open to the south and east, is easy from any direction. Most yachts enter Venezuela at Pampatar and then travel to Porlamar to take on cheap fuel and free fresh water from the town dock. Approach the anchorage by sailing inside Isla Blanco and rounding the headland at the east end of the bay, Morro de Punta Moreno. Behind this headland is the stone breakwater of a fishing dock and, impossible to miss by day or night, the imposing Concorde Hotel which is set back about half a mile from the point.

There are anchorages in the shallow, cloudy waters of the Bahia La Mar but the best anchorage is off the Concorde Hotel dock, about a mile from town.

Anchorage

Anchor in front of the Concorde Hotel and to the west of its two jetties in depths of about 3 metres in good holding greenish sand. The water is dirty, cloudy and green and does not invite swimming.

There are anchorages off the town dock but they are very bleak - the beach is filthy and the smell of rotting fish from the local market and spilt diesel from the fuel jetty is appalling. To approach the town dock keep out in the centre of the bay as there are shoals and rocks and the water is not clear. Line up the cathedral spire in the centre of Porlamar with the end of the dock. Approach slowly and carefully and go alongside only at the end of the dock where there is about 3 metres of water. The sea bed comes up very quickly away from the end of the dock. It should be possible to load supplies from the end of the dock.

Ashore

Leave your dinghy at the Concorde Hotel's dock by the tiny Marina Miguel. The Concorde has shops, taxis, telephones and telex; there are also 'Por Puesto' taxis, the Venezuelan equivalent of Martinique's collective taxis. Scuba Safaris is situated at the head of the marina dock and they stand by on VHF ch 68.

In Porlamar there are large supermarkets and numerous shops. The central focus of this large, bustling, and spread-out town is the Plaza Bolivar. Boulevard Guevara runs south of this square and is the major, pedestrian-only shopping precinct. A good supermarket is CADA. Most shops will take American dollars, as changing money can be a problem: not all banks have authorised bureaux de change. Numerous shops sell 'duty free' cigarettes (with a red stripe to emphasise that they are duty free) wines and spirits, and a few shops sell chandlery and fishing gear. There have been a series of reports of purchases of bad yacht varnish, yacht paint and antifouling. The tins were labelled with the names of well known manufacturers but the paints blistered or the antifouling dropped off after only a few months. The best and only real yacht chandlery is Off Shore Marine in Calle Marcano con Malave. There are ferry services from Porlamar to the mainland to Cumana and Puerto La Cruz.

An interesting voyage is an anticlockwise tour of Margarita Island.

The anchorages are quite comfortable and within easy reach of each other but the sea water is usually cloudy and greenish. After Pampatar the first stop would be Juangriego on northern Margarita.

Juangriego

Juangriego is a small town that caters for fishermen and tourists and is situated at the head of a gently shelving bay - Bahia San Juangriego. There is a fishermen's quay and a small town jetty.

Approach
Sail along the east coast of Isla Margarita; a mile offshore clears all dangers. Sail between Los Frailes islands and Cabo Negro which is lit (Fl 10s 235ft 12M). You can sail inside Isla Galera, but watch out for the large rock off Punta Galera which you should leave to port. A bay opens up to port, as you come south from Punta Galera, with a wreck in its north west corner and restaurants on the beach. This is not Bahia San Juangriego but there is a good anchorage in 3 to 4 metres of good holding sandy mud opposite the restaurants. The dinghy can be pulled up the beach and left in front of the largest restaurant if you wish to go ashore for an evening meal, but take care as swell with some breaking waves can build during the evening. The next bay south is the Bahia San Juangriego.

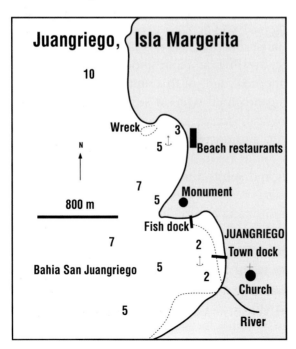

Anchorage
Enter the Bahia San Juangriego and anchor in depths of between 3 and 4 metres in good holding green sandy mud. There is a jetty in front of the town where you can leave the dinghy. The anchorage can be unpleasant in a northerly swell.

Ashore
This is a pretty town with an interesting church, a post office, shops, a bank and a number of restaurants, but the beach is dirty and there is a lot of traffic to and from the fish dock. A nearby fort is worth inspecting where, during the Venezuelan struggle for independence, the Spanish troops massacred the entire garrison after they had surrendered.

From the Bahia San Juangriego it is a pleasant day sail to the anchorage in the west of Margarita at Robledar.

Robledar

The anchorage is usually very uncrowded. It is not very scenic but it is sometimes used as stop-over for yachts heading north to Blanquilla Island.

Approach
Sail west across the Ensada La Guardia to Punta Tunar from Juangriego. The north coast of Margarita is flat and featureless but, as you cross the Ensada La Guardia, the twin peaks of the Picos de Maria Guevara (or Las Tetas) in the middle of the island, and the church at Juangriego, will enable you to fix your position. Some rocks stand out off the end of Punta Tunar and there is a light on a trestle at Morro Del Robledar (Fl 6s 40ft 11M).

Anchorage
Anchor in front of the small village among the fishing boats in depths of between 3 and 5 metres in good holding green sandy mud. The water is cloudy and the charts not very reliable so approach with care.

Ashore
A remote fishing village.

This is as far west as the guide goes. Isla Blanquilla and Isla Tortuga are easily accessible from Robledar as is Los Roques; these islands have some of the best anchorages in Venezuela, perhaps the Caribbean. But let us continue round the island of Margarita and back east, towards Trinidad and Tobago.

From Robledar head towards Punta Chigua. There are uncharted rocks and shoals that extend some two miles offshore and are difficult to spot in the murky, green water so make sure you give the coast a good offing. When you sail east along the southern coast of Margarita you will come to an anchorage in the Bahia Mangle, opposite the town of Boca Del Rio, or a better one further in the entrance to Laguana Grande in 3 to 4 metres of green sandy mud. However, there are rocks off the east side of the entrance and the area is full of mosquitoes.

It is interesting to visit the lagoons in the local boats, which come complete with sun awnings, for amongst the lagoon mangroves there is prolific bird life and there are waterways that lead right through the mangrove swamp to the north side of the island and a long beach, the Playa La Restinga, on the Ensenada La Guardia. If you do not wish to anchor off the lagoon, and I would not advise you to do so, this local boat trip through the lagoons can be arranged from Porlamar or Pampatar.

A more pleasant anchorage opposite Bahia Mangle, and just south of Margarita Island, is in the north east corner of Isla Cubagua.

Isla Cubagua

This is a sandy beached, dry, deserted island that was once an important pearl fishery. The first Spanish village in South America, Nueva Cadiz, was built in 1500 on Isla Cubagua but the village was totally destroyed by a violent earthquake in 1541.

Approach
This should present no problems *from any direction* except that a small shoal extends from the south east corner of the island. In the north east corner of the island there is a conspicuous wreck of a car ferry that went aground and caught fire some 20 years ago: the anchorage is south of the wreck. There is also an anchorage in the south west corner of the island behind a long sandy spit. There is a light on the northern point of the island (Fl 3s 29 ft 5M) and one in the middle of the north coast on Punta Palanquete.

Anchorage
Leave the wreck well to port and enter the bay to anchor close to the shore in 3 to 4 metres of clear water in fair holding sand.

Ashore
Nothing, except some pleasant walks.

There are also two anchorages on the next island east of Isla Cubagua, Isla Coche.

Isla Coche

The island was also once famous for its pearl fishery. Nowadays it is illegal, anywhere in Venezuela, to take oysters for pearls - fortunately it is not illegal to eat these delicious oysters. Although there are two good anchorages, Isla Coche is rarely visited by yachts. The best anchorage is off the western side of the island in a large crescent-shaped, sandy bay.

Approach
From the west beware of the shoal that extends about two miles off the north west of the island: the black buoy that is supposed to mark the shoal was missing in 1989. There is another unmarked shoal that is hard to see because of the cloudy water extending from the south west corner of the island off the small town of San Pedro.

Approaching Isla Coche *from the south east* watch out for a dangerous unmarked shoal that extends about half a mile from the south east corner of the island.

Anchorage
Off the crescent-shaped beach, you can anchor in the north part of the bay in sand in depths of between 3 and 4 metres. The charts are not very accurate around these Venezuelan islands so make sure that you voyage with care

Ashore
Nothing.

There is a second anchorage in the south of the island, opposite a white fisheries building and behind a long, low-lying spit. Because of the murky water the approach needs care. Slowly feel your way in with the depth sounder from the south west, make a note of your incoming course, and anchor in front of the white building behind the sandspit. The sandspit only becomes visible as you approach the shore. Anchor in depths of about 3 metres in good holding sandy mud. Ashore there is a small and friendly fishing community.

When leaving the southern anchorage head out on the reciprocal of the course you came in on until you reach depths of around 9 metres. If you intend to travel east through the passage between Isla Coche and Morro de Chacopata sail over towards Isla Los Lobos to avoid the shoals that extend off the south coast of Isla Coche. You can approach to within two miles of the coast of Isla Coche, but beware of the strong north westerly current that will push you very easily onto these offlying shoals.

The easterly voyage along the mainland coast of Venezuela is either a motor sail if you keep close to the shore or, if you have no engine, a series of long beats out to sea to find the wind. There is often a long swell that can between one and two metres high, sometimes more if there has been extensive hurricane activity in the north. The first easterly anchorage after Isla Coche is behind Punta Esmeralda.

Punta Esmeralda

There are actually two anchorages, one behind the Isla Esmeralda (100 metres high), but this anchorage is open to the swell, and the other more comfortable but less breezy anchorage in Esmeralda Bay.

Approach
From the west sail along the coast from Morro de Chacopata which is lit (Fl 15s 165ft 16M) and identify Isla Esmeralda before turning into the anchorages behind the island. On passage, Piedra Blanco (White Rock, 12 metres) some eight miles east of Morro de Chacopata, will help you fix your position.

Approaching *from the east* make sure you keep well outside the low rocky Islas Garrapatas, where the sea breaks, and which acts as a good landmark.

Anchorage
Drop the anchor behind Isla Esmeralda in a depth of some 6 metres in good holding black sandy mud. The local fishermen may ask you to move as they sometimes drive shoals of fish into their nets through

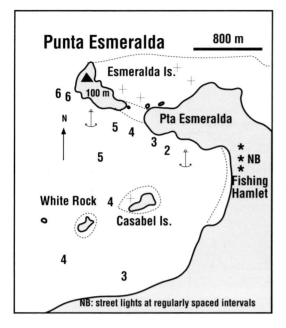

Punta Esmeralda   800 m

Esmeralda Is.

6 6 100 m

N

5 4

Pta Esmeralda

5   3 2

★ ★ NB ★
Fishing Hamlet

White Rock 4   Casabel Is.

4

3

NB: street lights at regularly spaced intervals

the gap between Isla Esmeralda and Punta Esmeralda.

The second anchorage is deeper into Ensada la Esmeralda, between the headland and the most eastern of the three tiny islands and towards the shore. If you arrive at dusk anchor in front of the regularly spaced street lights that lead up to the small fishing village. The bottom gently shelves from Punta Esmeralda and, as the water is a cloudy green, feel your way in with the depth sounder to anchor in a depth of about 2 metres in good holdingsticky black mud. The most western island (White Rock) clearly stands out from the shore.

Ashore
A poor fishing village.

Carupano

Carupano is some 15 miles east of Punta Esmeralda and generally used as a clearance port for yachts leaving Venezuela, but of course you could enter there if travelling west. There are a couple of large supermarkets and some yachts reprovision before heading back to the Windward Caribbean islands. The town is poor, the beach filthy, the dinghy and outboard should never be left unlocked and unattended, the authorities are heavy handed and the anchorage is open to northerly swells.

Approach
From the west there is a small 1.3 metre shoal that lies about a mile offshore between Punta Salinas and Carupano. Identify the harbour walls that run out from the town and the anchorage is to the west of

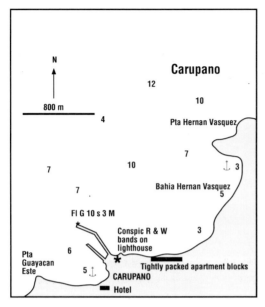

the western wall. At the end of the longest wall is a light (Fl G 10s 3M). To the east of the harbour and town are conspicuous tightly packed apartment blocks and in the town, behind the harbour, there is a large church with prominent spires. There should be a light on the quay (Fl 8 1/2s 12M).

Anchorage

In the bay south of the western wall anchor in 5 metres of cloudy water in good holding sand. There is no sign of the large mooring buoys marked on the British Admiralty charts. It is possible to go inside the harbour but it is usually crowded with local boats. Some yachts prefer to anchor in the northern corner of Bahia Hernan Vasquez behind the headland.

Ashore

There are a few small green parks and the people are friendly, but the town shops are a dreary twenty minutes walk away from the harbour and taxis are hard to find. It is possible to leave the dinghy on the beach in front of the park, but make sure you padlock everything, and secure and padlock the dinghy to a convenient tree.

Customs and Immigration

You have to clear (or enter) with the officials in the following order: coastguards on the main quay in the harbour; immigration a few streets away from the quay; customs on the main road towards the town; the Port Captain on the same road but further along. The coastguards will inspect your passport and point you in the right direction, but be prepared to have to pay about 600 or so bolivars (ask for the price regulations) and to spend a very hot frustrating morning.

There is a better sheltered but dirtier and smellier anchorage close to Carupano at the fish port of Puerto Santo. Yachts anchor in the West Bay, Bahia Oeste, where the smell of drying fish can be overpowering.

Puerto Santo

Puerto Santo, five miles east of Carupano, is the best anchorage between Esmeralda and the eastern end of the Paria Peninsula.

Approach
This should present no problem by day or by night.

Anchorage
Anchor in depths of 4 to 6 metres of filthy water in good holding oily black mud.

Ashore
At the southern fuel dock you can obtain water and diesel, with a depth of about 2.5 metres alongside. The town looks pretty from the mooring but the spit to the shore and windward beach are filthy (complete with a rotting dead dog when we were last there). There are a few basics in the shops, but it is possible to get a local taxi into Carupano to obtain supplies (and clear Venezuela) if you wish to stay at the more sheltered anchorage of Puerto Santo.

From Puerto Santo you could sail to Los Testigos and perhaps then up to Martinique. The alternative is to continue east along the mainland coast, but the anchorages are not much better than deep water coves. Also it is difficult to know exactly where you are as the mountainous steep-to tropical forest shore looks very much the same for nearly 100 miles. However, the winds are light along the coast and the only real problem is how to keep out of the swell.

The next easterly anchorage after Puerto Santo is under the lee of Punta Pargo in **Ensa Pargo** and it is probably best to leave Puerto Santo at dusk and make an overnight passage. There are only a few shore lights to help you fix your position and it will probably be a motor sail as the easterly wind usually dies at night.

At sun up close the coast. The five white rocks at the eastern end

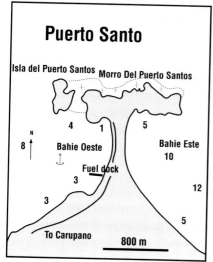

Puerto Santo

Isla del Puerto Santos — Morro Del Puerto Santos

Bahie Oeste

Bahie Este

Fuel dock

To Carupano

800 m

of **Ensenada Mejillones** should help you to fix your position. Off the next point, Punta la Ermita, there is a distinctive large rock with a hole through it, and about three miles further east is Ensa Pargo where there is an anchorage in the south east corner of the bay. Anchor off the beach with the houses and palm trees, in 8 metres in sand. A second anchor might help to cut down the roll.

The next bay, **Ensa San Francisco**, has an anchorage in its south east corner as does the next one, **Ensa Uquire,** which is behind Punta Uquire. Just off Punta Uquire there is a conspicuous island which looks as if it is made up of three large rocks. These three bays are difficult to identify from seaward and you need to be fairly close to the shore.

An alternative, if you do not like sailing too close to the shore in almost uncharted waters, is to round the Promontorio de Paria, the eastern tip of Venezuela, and enter the Gulf of Paria. Pass through the Boca Grande and drop anchor in the calm waters of **Ensenada Cariaquita**. Be careful of the rocks about half a mile off Punta Penas on the end of the peninsula, Garza Rocks (20 metres) and the rocks off Punta Garciatas when you turn to starboard to enter Ensenada Cariaquita. Keep to the middle of the bay and work your way through the murky water to drop anchor in a depth of about 3 metres. Wait for a fair wind to sail to Grenada from Ensenada Cariaquita.

You could also motor sail directly to Port of Spain without stopping on the Paria Peninsula.

Charts
British Admiralty: 1480 General, 230 Margarita, 493 Gulf of Paria, 1966 Los Roques
USA: 24420 General east, 24430 General west, 24423 Los Testigos, 24431 and 24432 Margarita
Imray Iolaire: D1 General, D25 Los Testigos, D211 Margarita, D11 A-D North coast

Radio Station, Frequency and Times of Weather Bulletin
Possibly Radio Antilles: 930 kHz (0800, 1830)

Airport
There is an airport on Isla Margarita that has connecter flights to the international airport of Maiquetia, close to Caracas on the mainland.

TRINIDAD and TOBAGO

Trinidad was discovered by Columbus in 1498 on his third attempt to discover a westerly route to the East Indies and China. Land was first sighted as three distinct hills; deeply-religious Columbus, who had placed the voyage under the protection of the Holy Trinity, named the island Trinidad. He called his landfall in the south east of the island Cabo de la Galera, because the headland looked from a distance like a galley with oars and pointed sails. The name of the headland has since, by a cartographer's error, been transferred to the north east corner of Trinidad and the original landfall is now known as Galeota Point. Columbus dropped anchor in Erin Bay on the south coast of Trinidad and to his horror found that instead of Chinese mandarins the island was inhabited by Arawak and Carib Indians.

England's Sir Walter Raleigh visited the island in 1595 on his long expedition to South America, and discovered the famous pitch lake - the result of oil running into a mud volcano. Trinidad was a Spanish colony from the 1500s but such an unsuccessful one that in 1780 Spain opened the island to settlers of all nations: within ten years the population grew from a few hundred to almost 20 000. Britain, for once without a fight, took over the island in 1797 and in 1802 Trinidad was officially ceded to Britain.

Tobago was discovered in 1498 but not settled until 1639 and, like Trinidad, was not particularly sought after by the Spanish colonists. The British effectively took Tobago at the same time as Trinidad and administratively joined it to Trinidad in 1809. Trinidad and Tobago remained British colonies until 1962 when they became a joint independent state within the British Commonwealth. In the following year a hurricane devastated Tobago, destroying much of the economy that was based on agriculture; since then it has increasingly turned to tourism.

In 1976 Trinidad and Tobago became a republic. Today oil and asphalt have replaced sugar and cocoa as the most important sectors of the economy, and recently reserves of offshore gas have been discovered. However, when the international demand for oil fell, the economy suffered and the country is now trying to diversify its economy and expand tourism.

Due to its colonial history Trinidad and Tobago has a complex, multiracial society - the majority of the inhabitants are Christians but there are many Muslims and Hindus among the 1.2 million population. Almost every continent has representatives living on Trinidad. The Amerindians were followed by the Spanish and their African slaves. The British brought in European labour and African slaves. Then from the mid 1800s, after the emancipation of the slaves and to relieve the shortage of labour, Britain imported East Indian and Chinese indentured labourers even as late as the early part of the twentieth century.

Trinidad and Tobago's multiracial society has not always been peaceful. In the last century, for example, the black recruits of the West Indian Regiment rebelled, but the leaders were captured by the British and cruelly tortured before being put to death. In this century, there was considerable unrest during the 1970s because of the Black Power movement, and in 1990 a revolutionary Muslim group stormed parliament, wounded and captured the Prime Minister and held him and his cabinet hostage. The revolution the Muslims expected did not happen, however, and they eventually surrendered.

Although Trinidad is one of the most violent of the Caribbean islands there is almost no history of acts of violence against tourists, and while parts of Port of Spain may run wild on a Saturday night, nearby Tobago is a quiet, peaceful backwater. Trinidad's carnival held in February/March is a wonderful event and always passes without problems. Many cruising yachts come to the island just to enjoy 'The Mas' (short for masquerade) - some of the more widely travelled believe The Mas matches Rio de Janeiro's carnival or the Mardi Gras in New Orleans.

Trinidad and Tobago has no well defined procedure for yacht entry and clearance. This, coupled with some really obstructive officials - notably in customs can often lead to long delays on entering and can give visiting yachts a bad first impression. In 1989, for example, some yachts were taking up to 10 hours to pass through Immigration, Port Authority and Customs at Port of Spain. After passing through the Bocas Del Dragon and entering the Gulf of Paria yachts used to be able to enter Trinidad and Tobago at Chaguaramas, to the west of Point Gourde, but nowadays yachts are being told to proceed to Port of Spain via the Grier Channel.

Port of Spain

Port of Spain is the capital and main port of Trinidad and Tobago, and is a lively, bustling, interesting town. Yachts have to enter Trinidad at Port of Spain.

Approach

If coming *from the north, west or east* there are no problems as the land is mountainous, steep to, and there are no offshore dangers. It is possible to enter (or leave) the Gulf of Paria through any of the bocas (mouths or channels) of the Bocas Del Dragon where the current generally runs in a north easterly direction and can be as strong as two and half knots. The sea off any of the bocas can be disturbed, owing to the currents and the amount of fresh water flowing out of the Gulf, but the wind is usually light. Approaching Trinidad *from a northerly or easterly direction* head for the most eastern boca - Boca de Monos - if you want the shortest trip to Port of Spain.

When coming *from Grenada* make allowance for the strong westerly-going South Equatorial Current that runs all along Trinidad's north coast and in the passage between Trinidad and Grenada. The lights of Trinidad and Tobago sometimes work, and the conspicuous powerful lighthouse (Fl 10s 26M) on the north of Chacachacare Island makes a good landfall. There is also a powerful light on Galera Point (Oc 10s 141ft 16M) on the tip of the north east coast. From Grenada aim to arrive off Boca Grande at dawn to pick up the Chacachacare light - you still have a good 15 miles to go before you arrive off Port of Spain. Rounding Chacachacare Island at dawn identify a second less powerful light on the island (Fl 2s 11M). When this light lines up with the lighthouse light on 036°True the transit clears Diamond Rock that lies off the south west corner of the island.

When *coming from the south* it is best to travel up the east coast of Trinidad and enter the Gulf of Paria through the Boca de Monos

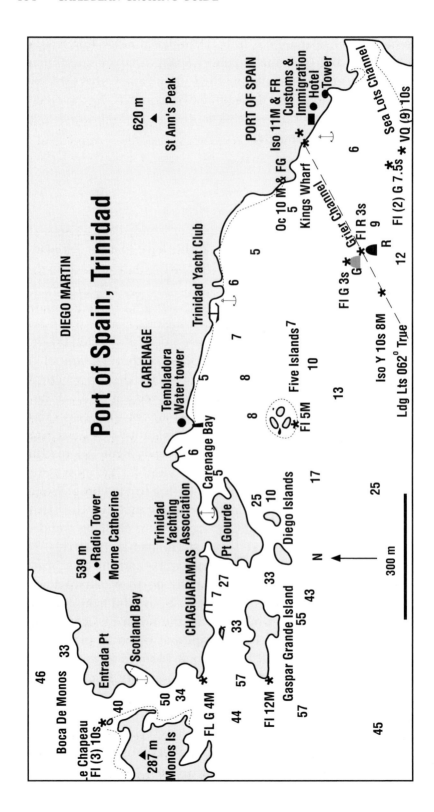

rather than attempt the entrance through the southern Serpent's Mouth and risk entanglement with the numerous oil rigs and   their attendant traffic.

Once through any of the bocas the safest course is outside Gaspar Grande Island and head for the Grier Channel passing Diego Islands and Five Islands to port. Grier Channel is deep and well lit (IALA system B - red right returning) and can be joined at any convenient point after Five Islands.

Anchorage

Head for the large hotel in the town and, when close, the unmarked customs and immigration dock. It is the wooden dock in front of a blue wooden building at the end of the conspicuous passenger ship wharf - King's Wharf. The customs and immigration dock lies north of the Trinidad - Tobago ferry terminal. If there is a space go alongside, otherwise anchor off in about 6 metres. The customs and immigration dock is high and thus not particularly safe for yachts, so if there is any sort of sea running anchor off and go ashore by dinghy.

You can leave the yacht at anchor off Port of Spain but I would not recommend it - the water is filthy, there is lots of local traffic and there have been break-ins. The best plan is to enter Trinidad at Port of Spain and then move straightaway, some three miles north west, to the Trinidad and Tobago Yacht Club Marina. Enter the marina by the west or east entrance or, if in doubt, anchor off outside the eastern entrance. There is a pleasant second anchorage some three miles further west of the Yacht Club Marina at Carenage Bay which is run by the Trinidad and Tobago Yachting Association.

Ashore

By Caribbean standards Port of Spain is a huge town. There are supermarkets, bars, restaurants, night clubs, many hotels and an interesting parliamentary building. At night parts of the down town area are 'no-go areas' - ask a reliable taxi driver for the safe parts of town. There are some 400 species of tropical birds on Trinidad and Tobago and a fascinating trip, which can be arranged through any of the major hotels, is to the Caroni Swamp Bird Sanctuary which is situated about three miles south of Port of Spain.

Cheap co-operative taxis run along the coast road that leads to the anchorages off the Yacht Club and the Yachting Association. Good pick up and set down points in Port of Spain are Independence Square and the corner of Park Street. There is an international airport, with regular flights to Europe and North and South America, just south of the town.

Customs and Immigration

At Port of Spain fill in the forms at the immigration office in the blue building behind the wooden wharf and then go to the tide surveyor's office and then the customs office in that order. They are all within walking distance of each other but failure to go in that order could result in long delays. The customs officer will probably insist that you go alongside the dock for a 'rummage' even if there is a nasty sea running and you have decided to anchor off - it is up to you how you respond. If you have firearms to declare they have to be deposited with the police and that can take an hour or so. The customs and Excise Division have two unpleasant rules for cruising yachts. One, that vessels are 'not to be removed from their point of anchorage without the prior approval of the proper customs officer' and two, that 'permission must be given by the customs officer for visitors to board vessels'.

When leaving Trinidad you have to go through it all again: immigration, tide surveyor and customs, and yachts that carry firearms and ammunition, should give customs at least 24 hours' notice of departure time so they can organise their return. When you inform customs that you intend to go to the marina at the Trinidad and Tobago Yacht Club the officer will tell you to report to the customs post at Chaguaramas - about five miles away by road from the yacht club. You can take a bus or a taxi from outside the yacht club. (When you arrive at Chaguaramas customs post, however, be prepared for the customs officer to be at a loss as to how to respond).

Trinidad and Tobago Yacht Club

Approach

The yacht club can be contacted on VHF ch 68 and it is marked on British Admiralty chart 483 as an 'upside down T' about two miles east of Tembladora. At night a powerful yellow security light shines out from the marina. The entrance to the marina's fuel and fresh water dock is through the western entrance behind a sunken wreck which is used as part of the harbour wall. Keep to the centre of the entrance channel, which should have a depth of 3 metres in the middle, and once inside keep away from the slipway to the north of the fuel dock as the bottom comes up rapidly. Go alongside the dock and obtain a berth number. This will probably mean leaving by the western entrance and re-entering by the eastern entrance.

Anchorage
The anchorage is in depths of 4 to 7 metres off the eastern entrance - keep an eye out for the small half-sunken buoys as you approach.

Alongside and Ashore
The marina will take yachts over 15 metres long and drawing up to 3 metres (most berths are filled with local power boats) and each berth has free electricity and water. For a 45 ft (13.7 metres) boat the berthing fees are around $200 US per month or $0.36 US per ft per day. The marina is usually full at carnival time but a berth can be reserved by writing to: The Manager, The Trinidad Yacht Club, Baphore Cocorite, Port of Spain, Trinidad and Tobago, West Indies. You join the club for a small fee and you are able to use all its facilities which include a restaurant and bar as well as fresh water showers.

The club members are very helpful and the club management can arrange for a sailmaker, marine electronics, wood workers and a diesel mechanic. Some local shops just outside the entrance sell all the basics, and buses and collective taxis run regularly to Port of Spain, or to a huge shopping mall some distance before the capital, where there are supermarkets, boutiques, banks and travel agents.

Trinidad and Tobago Yachting Association

The Trinidad and Tobago Yachting Association is the yachting centre of Trinidad. The Association has laid a number of moorings in Carenage Bay, built a club house, runs a boatyard, organises races and welcomes visiting cruising yachts to share their facilities. The Association can be called on VHF ch 68 from 1000 - 1230 and 1600 - 1900, but try outside these hours as you may be lucky and get a reply.

Approach
From the west, pass between the Point Gourde on the mainland and the northernmost of the Diego Islands. The bay is tucked away round

Point Gourde. Coming *from the east* it is about three miles due west from the Trinidad and Tobago Yacht Club marina.

Anchorage

Anchor in about 5 metres in front of the moorings and go ashore to meet the management. There is sometimes a possibility of a visitor's mooring.

Ashore

The anchorage is secure and safe and there is a dinghy dock, a club house, a bar, toilets and showers. The Association's management likes to interview visiting skippers before they offer their facilities for a length of stay of two weeks, but this can be extended. There is a 15-ton travel lift and a secure boatyard where storage costs $5.0 US per ft for the first week and then $0.50 US per ft per day. You can work on your own boat but there is no chandlery and Port of Spain is almost 10 miles away. Taxis park outside the entrance to the Association and there is a regular bus service. The Association members are extremely helpful and friendly and understand the needs of cruising yachts.

The anchorage in Carenage Bay is a good point of departure for yachts wishing to visit Tobago. You have to clear Trinidad from Port of Spain but at least you do not have to take the boat - skippers can go to town by bus and take passports and ship's papers through immigration, tide surveyor and customs.

There are other anchorages in Trinidad at **Scotland Bay** south of Entrada Point in the Boca de Monos and in the south east of Chacachacare Island but the water in the Gulf and the Bocas is always cloudy and sometimes oily. Around Tobago, however, the sea is usually clear and blue and the sands are golden - the only problem is getting there.

Tobago

After entering the Republic of Trinidad and Tobago at Port of Spain you have to re-enter Trinidad and Tobago at Scarborough if you wish to visit Tobago - even though you never leave territorial waters. Further, you *have* to go to Scarborough even though it is a dangerous sail from Port of Spain (because of Wasp Shoal) and an unsafe yacht haven. It would be more sensible to sail to the safer anchorage in

Store Bay and then take ship's papers and crew list by road to Scarborough, but the officials have decided otherwise.

The easiest way to arrive in Tobago is from Barbados, perhaps after a transatlantic voyage. The 140-mile trip is an exhilarating, trade wind powered reach.

Approach

When approaching Tobago *from any direction* there is a powerful radiobeacon just north of the airport in the south west of the island (TAB, 323 kHz, 100 miles) which will help with the landfall. The passage to Tobago from Trinidad is easiest in the summer months when the winds tend to be light and from the south east, and it helps if you have a reliable motor for the trip along the north coast. A possible winter sail to Tobago would be from Vieux Fort in the south of Saint Lucia. Local yachts regularly sail to Tobago from Trinidad in the spring for a week of racing.

The voyage *from Trinidad to Tobago* is never easy. There is a strong two to three knot north westerly current flowing through the Galleons Passage between Tobago and Trinidad, and just south of Crown Point is a dangerous shoal, Wasp Shoal, which has less than 2 metres of water.

If approaching Tobago *from the west* in the summer time, leave Trinidad at dusk and head through the Boca de Monos to the Galleons Passage. The winds tend to die at night so you will probably have a sloppy motor sail along the north coast of Trinidad. Keep as close to the coast as possible and head for Corozal Point and then Saut d'Eau Island which is supposed to be lit (Fl 5s 14M). If there is too much contrary wind or the swell is too high you can always return through the Boca de Monos which is lit at the north western end (Fl (3) 10s) and the south eastern end (Fl G 4s 4M). Once outside the boca work your way about two miles offshore along the north coast; it is steep-to and there are few offlying dangers. Do not expect the lights to work and there are no well protected anchorages.

Some local yachts put in to Chupara Bay, behind Chupara Point and the reef that extends from the point, but the anchorage is often unpleasant because of the roll, and in the winter months it is usually untenable because of the northerly swell. Head east along the north coast of Trinidad past Grand Matelot Point and aim for Galera Point which is lit (Oc 10s 141ft 16M). If you cruise at around or less than five knots, the further east you go the better before you turn to port for Tobago. The aim is to keep out of the westerly running current in the Galleons Passage (which is weaker the closer you are to Trinidad's north coast) and to keep clear of shallow Wasp Shoal which is unmarked and difficult to see.

As you head out into Galleons Passage expect the wind to increase in strength from out of the east, and the current to be at least two knots. If you can make Scarborough without being swept down onto Wasp Shoal all well and good, but if you find you are being pushed away to leeward, head for Crown Point which is lit (Fl (4) 20s 115ft 11M). Avoid Wasp Shoal and head up into Store Bay off Milford Bay just north of the airport. Drop the anchor and recover your strength before tackling the 12-mile beat along Tobago's southern coast, against a strong wind and current, to Scarborough. Make sure you give Crown Point and the next point, Columbus Point, a clearance of at least a mile.

Store Bay

Store Bay off Milford Bay is the best anchorage in Tobago. There are white sanded beaches, there is good swimming and it is a convenient spot from which to explore Buccoo Reef and visit the rest of the island.

Approach
From Scarborough give Bulldog Shoal and Columbus and Crown Points a good clearance. There is a sectored light in the middle of Store Bay (Q WRG 23 ft 5.4M); the white sector is the safe sector. In the north of Milford Bay the yellow and black Cardinal West (V Q(9) 10s) and Cardinal North (Q) buoys that mark Buccoo Reef are clearly visible.

Anchorage
In the south of Milford Bay, that lies between Pigeon Point and Sandy Point, is small Store Bay.   As you approach Store Bay you will see a sign warning you not to anchor near the submarine cables that run out from the land just north of the light. Anchor in the middle of Store Bay in front of the light (which is not easily seen) and off the beach in a depth of about 6 metres in good holding sand. There are some distinctive storage tanks on the north side of Sandy Point and palm trees line the beach south of Pigeon Point.

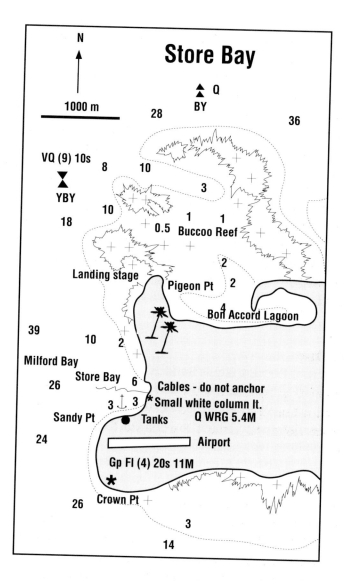

Store Bay

N

1000 m

Q
BY

28

36

VQ (9) 10s

8   10

3

YBY

10   1   1

18   0.5 Buccoo Reef

2

Landing stage

Pigeon Pt   2

Bon Accord Lagoon

39   4

10   2

Milford Bay

Store Bay   6

26   Cables - do not anchor

3 3 Small white column lt.

Sandy Pt   Q WRG 5.4M

24   Tanks

Airport

Gp Fl (4) 20s 11M

26   Crown Pt

3

14

Ashore

There are hotels, with bars and restaurants, where you can hire a car. You can also hire cars at the nearby airport or at Scarborough, which is only half an hour away by bus. A scuba diving shop is situated at the north end of the beach. To visit Buccoo Reef take the dinghy up past Pigeon Point where there is a landing stage, or alternatively take a reef excursion in one of the glass-bottomed boats which work out of Store Bay.

It might be possible to take a yacht through Buccoo Reef, although I have not tried it. The entrance is north of the Cardinal West buoy and depending on your draft and the state of the tide it might just be possible to reach Bon Accord Lagoon where there are supposed depths of around 5 metres off Sheerbird Point. The Bon Accord Lagoon is Tobago's only possible hurricane hole, but if there is any chance of a hurricane (and this is extremely unlikely as, although Tobago was hit in 1963, it was only its second hurricane in recorded history) I would suggest that you sail to the south coast of Grenada, which is only about 80 miles away and where there are some excellent hurricane holes.

Scarborough

The capital of Tobago, and the only point of entry, is situated at the head of Rockley Bay. The anchorage is uncomfortable as swell enters the bay. Ferries regularly travel between Port of Spain and Scarborough, so the harbour is well lit.

Approach
South west of Rockley Bay is Bulldog Shoal where the sea breaks. The shoal is marked by a lit, yellow and black Cardinal South buoy (V Q (6) + L Fl 10s). When entering Rockley Bay there is a green, lit buoy (Fl G 3s) which has to be left to port. Off Bacolet Point there is a red, lit buoy (Fl R 3s) which has to be left to starboard, as does the lit (Fl Y 2.5s) yellow buoy off Minister Rock. By day there are two (difficult to see) triangles which line up for the entrance transit and by night two lights, the lower one sectored (Oc 5s 33ft 11M and Iso WRG 2s 16 ft 7-5 M) and the safe sector is white. There is a powerful light tower (Gp Fl (2) 20s 463 ft 29M) situated just south of Fort George and nearby there are several radio masts. The south wall of the ferry harbour at Scarborough is lit (Q R 18ft 2M) and there is another pylon light just west of the dock (Q G 18ft 2M).

Anchorage
Anchor south of the ferry harbour wall in about 3 metres. It is sometimes possible to take on water on the ferry dock, and you could try to come alongside just for the entrance formalities if the berth is clear of ferries.

Ashore
There are supermarkets and a vegetable market.

Customs and Immigration
Go first to immigration on the west side of the bay and then to customs. Customs, for some reason only known to themselves, are currently restricting yachts to the anchorages at Store Bay and Man of War Bay. Store Bay is a good anchorage and nearby is the fabulous Buccoo Reef.

Man of War Bay

This is a huge bay on the north coast of Tobago, perhaps more fun to visit by land than by sea.

Approach
Approach along the north coast of Tobago. You can sail inside The Sisters. Enter below North Point and there is a sectored light from the town of Charlotteville (Q WRG 82 ft 5-4M). The white sector is the safe sector;   green shines over the rocks south of North Point.

Anchorage
Anchor in the north east corner of the bay. The bottom comes up steeply, anchor in sand in depths of about 7 metres.

Ashore
There are basics in the village.

Charts
British Admiralty: 956 General Caribbean, 493 General Trinidad and Tobago, 483 Gulf of Paria - East, 484 Bocas del Dragon, 505 Tobago
USA: 24401 General Trinidad, 24402 Tobago, 24404 Gulf of Paria and Peninsula

Radio Station, Frequency and Times of Weather Bulletin
Local radio stations

Airports
There is an International Airport on Trinidad situated just to the east of Port of Spain. On Tobago there is also an airport near Store Bay which has some international flights and there are regular flights to Trinidad. Tel: 664 8047

Marinas, Boatyards and Sail Lofts

Location	Min depth Max length	Water (W), Fuel (F), Elect (E)	Haul out facilities refer to: maximum displacement (tons), maximum keel (m), maximum length (m)
ANTIGUA			
Nelson's Dockyard, English Harbour Tel: 463 1053 VHF: 68	3m 20+m	W, E	Well sheltered, reasonably priced marina, but often overcrowded in season. Moor stern-to. A&F Sails (Tel: 31522. VHF: 68). Nelson's Dockyard. Antigua Sails (Tel: 31527 VHF: 68), close to Dockyard.
Antigua Slipway, English Harbour Tel: 463 1056 VHF: 68/12	2.5m 20+ m	W, F, E	Moor alongside; a comprehensive chandlery. There are two haul out facilities in the yard but you cannot work on your own boat. Travel lift: 35T, 2.1m, 15m. Rail haul: 125T 3.7m, 30m.
Cat Club Marina, Falmouth Harbour Tel: 463 1036 VHF: 68/14/16	4m 20+ m	W, F, E	Well sheltered marina which is often full.
Antigua Yacht Club Marina, Falmouth Harbour Tel: 463 1444 VHF: 68/16	3m 20+ m	W, E	A new marina project just under way in well-sheltered Falmouth Harbour.
St James Club, Mamora Bay Tel: 463 1430 VHF: 68	3m 20+ m	W, F, E	Exclusive resort. Marina berths often filled with motor boats.
Crabbs Marina & Slipway, Parham Tel: 463 2113 VHF: 68/16	5m 20+ m	W, F, E	Well sheltered and reasonably priced marina and yard. Work on your own boat and good facilities. Close to the international airport and St John's. Travel lift: 50 T, 3m, 15m. Crane.
BARBADOS			
Boatyard, Bay St, Bridgetown Tel:424806/41	No marina	W	An open anchorage but crane haul-out possible in Bridgetown Commercial Harbour: inquire at the Boatyard. Sail repairs possible, again inquire at the Boatyard.
BEQUIA			
Bequia Marina, Admiralty Bay Tel: 45 83272 VHF: 68/16	No marina	W, F, E	Possible to overnight at the small fuel dock. Not a very active yard and not very cheap but reasonable facilities. Rail haul: 100T, 3m. Lincoln Simmons sail loft near Bosun's Locker chandlery.
CARRIACOU			
Carriacou Boat-Builders, Tyrell Bay Tel: 37542 VHF: 16	No marina	W, E	A new yard which makes and sells aluminium dinghies. Aluminium and steel welding. Rail haul: 100T, 2.9m, 25m. Possibility of sail and awning repairs.

Marinas, Boatyards and Sail Lofts

Location	Min depth Max length	Water (W), Fuel (F), Elect (E)	Haul out facilities refer to: maximum displacement (tons), maximum keel (m), maximum length (m)
GRENADA			
Grenada Yacht Services, St George's Tel:4402548 VHF: 16	3m 2m	W, F, E	Marina in a state of decay but there are moves to regenerate the decaying pontoons. Yard active but somewhat run down. Two haul facilities - Synchrolift: 200T; Screw Dock: 20T, 3.5m, 15m.
Yacht Club, The Lagoon, St George's	No marina		Rail haul: 10T, 1.8m, 4m. Rail haul in need of repair.
Spice Island Marine Services Tel: 444 4257/4342 VHF:16	3m 25m	W, F, E	Attractive marina for 25 yachts moored stern-to. A clean yard with good facilities and you can work on your own boat. Travel lift: 35T, 3 m. A sail loft is attached to the yard.
GUADELOUPE			
Bas du Fort Marina, Pointe à Pitre Tel: 908485 VHF: 16/9	2.2m 35m	W, F, E	First class facilities at the reasonably priced marina and yard. You can work on your own boat. Travel lift: 27T, 3.5m. Dove Sails (Tel: 841435), English agent for North Sails. For awnings try Caraibes Covering (Tel: 902497).
Chantier Lemaire, Pointe à Pitre Tel: 903447/901011	No marina	W, E	Well equipped yards and you can work on your own boat. Good for multi-hulls. Dry dock: 80T, 3m, 10m. Floating dock: 700T. Crane 15T.
Chantier Forbin, Pointe à Pitre Tel: 832134/52	No marina	W, E	Oldest established yard in Guadeloupe. Rail hauls: 20T, 2m.
Marina Rivière Sens, Courbeyre, Nr Basse Terre Tel: 817761 VHF:16	3m 20m	W, F, E	Usually full with local boats. Very reasonably priced marina.
St François Marina, Grand Terre Tel: 844728	2.5m	W, F, E	Difficult to approach and usually full with local boats. Few facilities.
ILES des SAINTES			
Marigot Bay, Iles des Saintes, Terre d'en Haut Tel: 995315	No marina	W, F, E	Reasonable facilities but isolated from town. Rail haul: 110T, 3.1 m, 33 m.

Marinas, Boatyards and Sail Lofts

Location	Min depth Max length	Water (W), Fuel (F), Elect (E)	Haul out facilities refers to : maximum displacement (Tons), maximum keel (m), maximum length (m)
MARTINIQUE			
Pointe du Bout Marina Tel: 660774 VHF: 9	3m 18m	W, E	Marina is usually full with local boats. Reasonably priced if you can obtain a berth.
Avimer/Bakoua, Anse Mitan Tel: 660545 VHF: 16	4 m 20+ m	W, F, E	Mooring stern-to Bakoua pontoon but open to a westerly swell. Often full with large charter yachts. Sail loft: Voilerie Artisanale (Tel: 660158) at Anse Mitan. English spoken.
Ship Shop, Quai Ouest, Fort de France Tel:737399	No marina	W, F, E	First class facilities. Price reasonable and work on your own boat. Travel lift: 30T, 4m, 24m. Chandlery, Fort de France. Sail lofts: West Indies Sails, Quai Ouest (Tel: 630408), English spoken. Also Helenon Ralph (Tel: 602205), Fort de France.
SIGBR Dry Dock, Quai Ouest, Fort de France Tel: 726940	No marina	W, E	Dry dock: Arrange to enter with a large ship.
Grant's, Baie des Tourelles, Tel: 702181	No marina	W, E	Old established yard but shallowing near the haul. Rail haul: 35T, 2m, 20m.
Club Nautique, Marin. Tel: 748533 VHF: 9	2.5m, 16m	W, E	A few bow-on temporary berths on the quay wall, often full with local boats. Well sheltered.
SAINT LUCIA			
Rodney Bay Marina Tel: 45 20324/447/314 VHF: 16	3m, 25m	W, F, E	First class facilities at the marina and the yard. Prices reasonable and work on your own boat. Travel lift: 50T, 3m, 20m. Stevens Yachts also offer some facilities. Sail maker: Topsail (Tel: 27773, VHF: 16). Also the possibility of sail repairs at Stevens Yachts in the marina complex.
Castries Yacht Services, Castries Tel: 26234/25348 VHF: 16	No marina	W, F, E	Good facilities at the yard and prices reasonable but situated a long way from town. Work on your own boat. Travel lift: 30T, 3m, 20m.
Marigot Bay Marina, Marigot Bay Tel: 45 343357 VHF: 16	2.5m 14m	W, F, E	A few marina berths available. Marigot Bay is full of charter yachts and has few facilities.
SAINT VINCENT			
Calliaqua Bay Yard Tel: 84214	No marina	W, E	Not a very active yard. Rail Haul: 15T, 2.3m, 25m.

Marinas, Boatyards and Sail Lofts

Location	Min depth Max length	Water (W), Fuel (F), Elect (E)	Haul out facilities refer to: maximum displacement (tons), maximum keel (m), maximum length (m)
TRINIDAD & TOBAGO			
Yacht Club, Baphore Cocorite Tel: 637 4260 VHF: 68/16	3m 18m	W, F, E	Marina sometimes full with local boats. Airy and reasonably priced for short or long term stay. No yard. Sailmaker: inquire at office or club bar!
Yachting Association, Carenage Bay Tel: 634 4376 VHF: 68/16	No marina	W	Yard some distance from Port of Spain; few facilities but pleasant surroundings. Work on your own boat. Travel lift: 15T, 2.5m, 12m.
UNION			
Anchorage Yacht Club, Union Island Tel: 458221/8424	No marina	W, F, E	Make sure that the hauls are working. Fresh water can be scarce and the yard has almost no facilities. Two rail hauls: 6T & 30T, 2m.
VENEZUELA			
Cumana Marina, Cumana, Venezuela Tel: 093 22103	Inquire	W	Marina and yard often full. Rail haul at Vanadero Caribe (093 662564).

INDEX